A Day in the Life of Australia

This book is dedicated to Olivier Rebbot

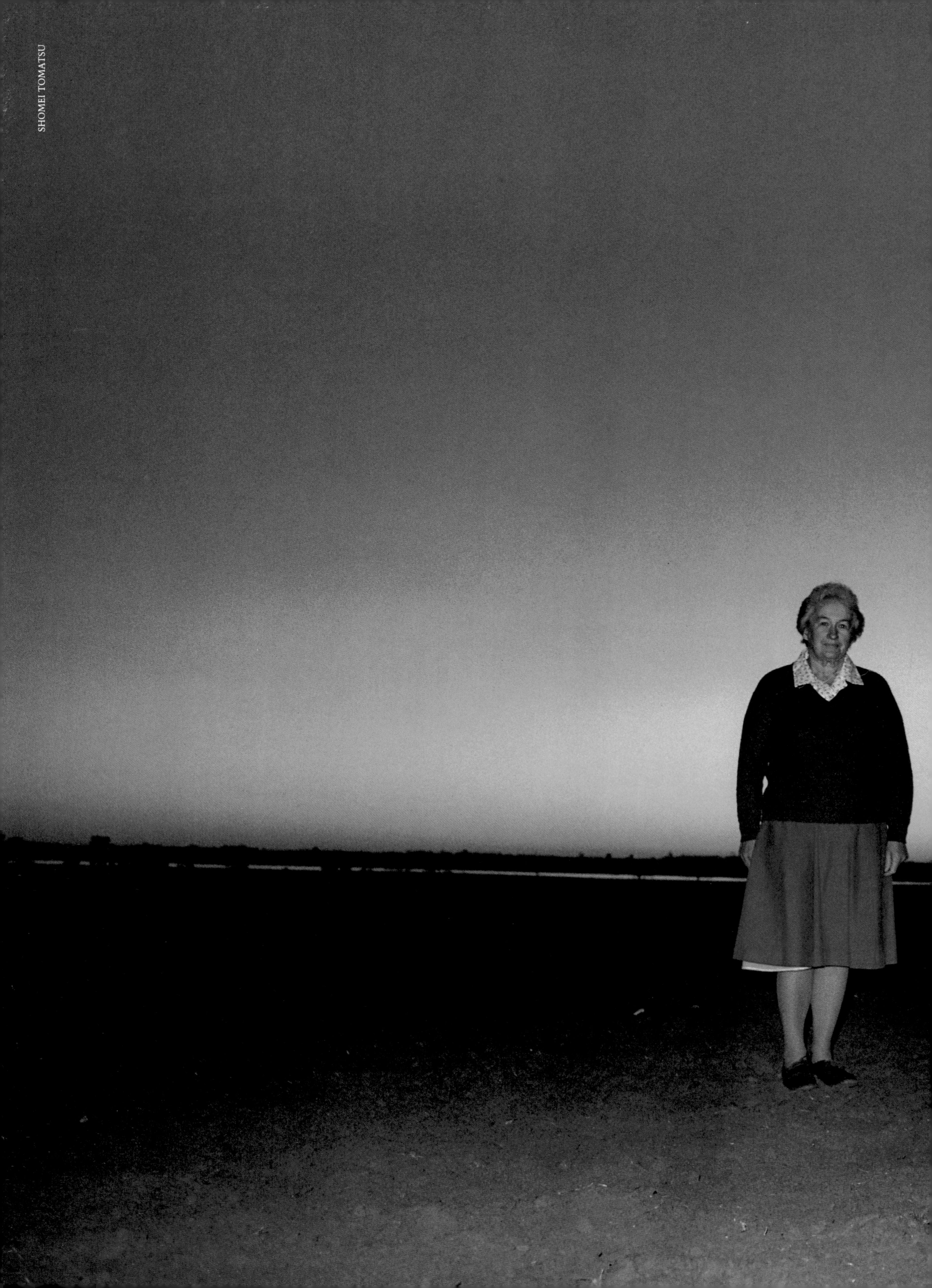

SHOMEI TOMATSU

5.45 am
Friday March 6, Natimuk, Victoria.

In the first light of day Japanese photographer Shomei Tomatsu records Tim and Marion Boehm standing in their fallow wheat fields.

This book would not have been
possible without the assistance
of the following Corporations:

Trans Australia Airlines

A Day in the Life of Australia

Photographed by 100 of the world's leading Photojournalists

March 6, 1981

First Published in Sydney, Australia 1981
Printed and bound in Australia for:
A DAY IN THE LIFE OF AUSTRALIA
Pty. Ltd.

First Published in the United States of
America 1982
Distributed by Harry N. Abrams, Inc.,
New York; ISBN 0-8109-1801-3;
Library of Congress Catalog Card Number
for First Printing: 81-195438

First Published in Canada 1982
Distributed by William Collins Sons &
Company, Toronto

First Published in the United Kingdom 1982
Distributed by Mitchell Beazley,
London, Limited

© DITLA 1981

National Library of Australia
Cataloguing-in-Publication Entry

A Day in the Life of Australia

ISBN 0-9594244-0-7

 I. Photography, Artistic
II. Australia—Social life and customs—
    Pictorial works
 I. Park, Andy. II. Smolan, Rick
    779.9994'06'3

Project Directors: Rick Smolan and
Andy Park

Black and white photographs for reproduction
printed on Ilford Galerie paper by Leanne
Temme/J.B.G. Photographic Laboratories,
Melbourne
Ektachrome processing by Vision Graphics,
North Sydney
Color separations by Dai Nippon, Tokyo
Printed in Ballarat Superfine Art supplied
by APPM
Photosetting by The Typographers,
Artamon, NSW
Printed by Griffin Press Limited, Adelaide
Photographs shot on Kodak Film
A Kevin Weldon Production

MIKE O'BRIEN

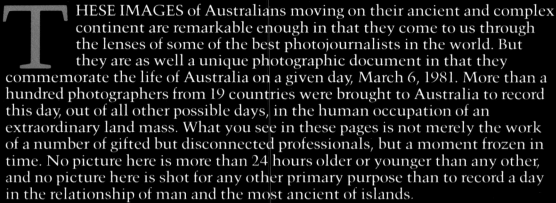

Introduction

THESE IMAGES of Australians moving on their ancient and complex continent are remarkable enough in that they come to us through the lenses of some of the best photojournalists in the world. But they are as well a unique photographic document in that they commemorate the life of Australia on a given day, March 6, 1981. More than a hundred photographers from 19 countries were brought to Australia to record this day, out of all other possible days, in the human occupation of an extraordinary land mass. What you see in these pages is not merely the work of a number of gifted but disconnected professionals, but a moment frozen in time. No picture here is more than 24 hours older or younger than any other, and no picture here is shot for any other primary purpose than to record a day in the relationship of man and the most ancient of islands.

It is not possible nor desirable that an introduction cover the complexities of Australian society or history. But when you look at these pictures it might serve to remember a few connected facts. The continent of Australia has not been as long occupied as others. The Aboriginal races have lived in Australia for somewhere between 30 and 50 thousand years. In the life of mankind, this is but a day. The Europeans have been here less than 200 years, a mere heartbeat. European society commenced in Australia almost involuntarily and with bad grace. The first Europeans were administrators, or the military, or chained convicts under sentence. On a fiercely humid day in 1788 they came to a port as strange and as remote to them as Mars would be to us.

There has always been this sense of strangeness, of other worldliness to the Australian continent, and as in the case of many a new nation, an aspect of desperate choice in the immigration of people to Australia. Even the Aborigines, who seem to possess a profound connection with the Australian land, were driven here from Indonesia by a New Stone Age people. Others, much later, were forced here by the Industrial Revolution, by land hunger and sundry economic, political and social pressures. All commenced their own heroic and bemusing adaptation to the Australian continent.

So the people you observe and become involved with in the pages of this unique chronicle are—with the exception of the Aboriginals—relative newcomers. If they walk over the surface of the continent with apparent confidence it is a tribute to human powers of adaptation. Despite the diversities of their histories, they have all formed a connection with the unearthly, aloof, sublime spectacle that is Australia.

The camera, unlike the first and often confused European settlers, is just as much at home in a rational landscape as in a surreal one, in an ordered garden as in an intimidating wilderness. I would not like to imply that the photograph is not an art form, but its art derives from the photographer's selection of time and frame. Within the frame itself, the camera brings an attitude of neutrality to a place, a time, a person. In the neutrality of these photographs is their truth. In their professional brilliance is their art, their charm, their delight.

Thomas Keneally

"A Day in the Life of Australia"

November 5, 1980

Dear Photographer,

I'm writing to tell you about a project I'm in the process of organising here in Australia. I'm an American freelance photographer, and for the past few years I've been working in Asia and Australia for several magazines – TIME, Fortune, New York Times, GEO, etc. During that time I spent eight months in the Australian outback photographing a young woman's 1,700 mile camel trek through the Gibson Desert for National Geographic Magazine.

In between assignments, I've been organising a project in which I hope to bring 70 of the world's best photographers to Australia in early March 1981, and combine them with 30 top Australian photographers. The basic idea is to distribute the 100 photographers all over Australia and give everyone the same 24-hour period to capture a typical Australian day on film. The results of the 24-hour shoot will be a hardcover 300-page book to be titled 'A Day in the Life of Australia'.

The biggest problem my Australian partner Andy Park and I have encountered has obviously been financing the mission. The two of us have invested all our savings (all $11,000 of it) to raise enough money to run the project (a mere million dollars!). In the past nine months we've met with over 400 companies asking them to help. It's been nearly impossible to get cash but several companies have offered services – like international and domestic airfares, hotel rooms, film, office space, communication facilities, etc. We've also been fortunate in having a lot of friends who have offered to help set up the arrangements for the photographers in each of the seven Australian states. We've managed to find families willing to offer their homes and hospitality. Even though the day of shooting (Friday March 6) is 'The Day' each photographer will have several days in his location to research his assignment.

We are also planning to do a 60-minute TV documentary using the project as a way to show how photographers work. In addition we are setting up a photographic seminar in Sydney so all the photographers can have the opportunity to meet and look at each other's work for a few days before the real work begins. If it sounds like a massive juggling act, you're right! At the moment Andy and I are going crazy trying to get everything organised within our deadlines.

The aim of this project is not to make THE definitive statement about Australia. The goal is to capture a slice of life on a typical day. We've chosen a Friday because it combines a workday with the beginning of the weekend's activities.

While we will be giving specific assignments, obviously each photographer will be free to branch off and photograph anything that seems relevant to the idea of what a typical day is like here – the assignment is just a starting point. Whatever you discover during the day is up to you – all we ask is that you make great pictures!

Although the project has the support of the Australian Government, several tourist organisations and a number of private companies, this is not a public relations exercise or a tourist promotion. It's not going

...../2

to be a book of 'picture postcards'. We've exp ___ ___ everyone ___
the project that the photographers invited to par ___ ___ are journalists
and we've accepted no outside editorial control over what you shoot or
what ends up in the book.

There isn't even a guarantee that every photographer will get a
photograph in the book. That decision is totally up to the picture editors
and depends on whether or not you have a good day on March 6.

Once the project is over we hope that you will use this opportunity to
work on your own projects or obtain other assignments here in Australia for
the publications you normally supply with photographs.

If you are interested in being part of this crazy idea, here are a few
things we need from you quickly and some information for your reference:

a. Biography: Don't be modest. We need as much info about your photo
    career as possible. Awards, exhibits, books published, major magazine
    stories, etc. We would also appreciate a good photo of you - in action
    if possible.

b. Film: We will supply you with 30 rolls of 35mm film (Tri-X, Kodachrome
    or Ektachrome). It would help us to know your requirements in advance.

c. Automobiles: In most cases you will be provided with a rental car, or
    if you prefer, a car with driver.

d. Insurance: Although the project is insured with public liability (i.e.
    if you drop a camera on the mayor's daughter's head we are covered),
    we will not be able to insure you personally. Your own insurance must
    cover you.

e. Room-mates: If you take advantage of our hotel accommodation during
    the four days you stay in Sydney, you will share a twin room with a
    famous photographer at absolutely no extra cost to you.

f. Payment: There isn't any. Depending on the sale of the book any
    profits will be shared between the photographers, the staff, and Andy
    and myself.

We will be sending out more specific information to each photographer
in the near future but this letter is to ask if the idea interests you?
Thanks for taking the time to consider coming down here to work with us on
'A Day in the Life of Australia'.

Andy and I will be looking forward to hearing from you.

Regards,

Rick Smolan

RICK SMOLAN

P.S.

Please excuse the "form letter" invitation —
you can imagine what it's like trying to
co-ordinate 100 photographers. I hope you'll
consider helping us with the project. I don't
know if you've ever been to Australia, but it
has the most unbelievable light I've ever seen —
must be the lack of pollution in the Southern
Hemisphere or something — the air has an
iridescent shimmer to it around twilight.
Totally unlike anything I've ever seen
(hope I've managed to intrigue you!)

Rick

The Tea and Sugar Train rests at the
Kingoonya Siding, South Australia.
This unique train provides a weekly
service to the isolated families living
along the 1048 km stretch of track
between Port Augusta and Kalgoorlie.
The carriages include a post office, a
butcher, and a grocery store. It will
soon be open for business.

Sydney Harbour

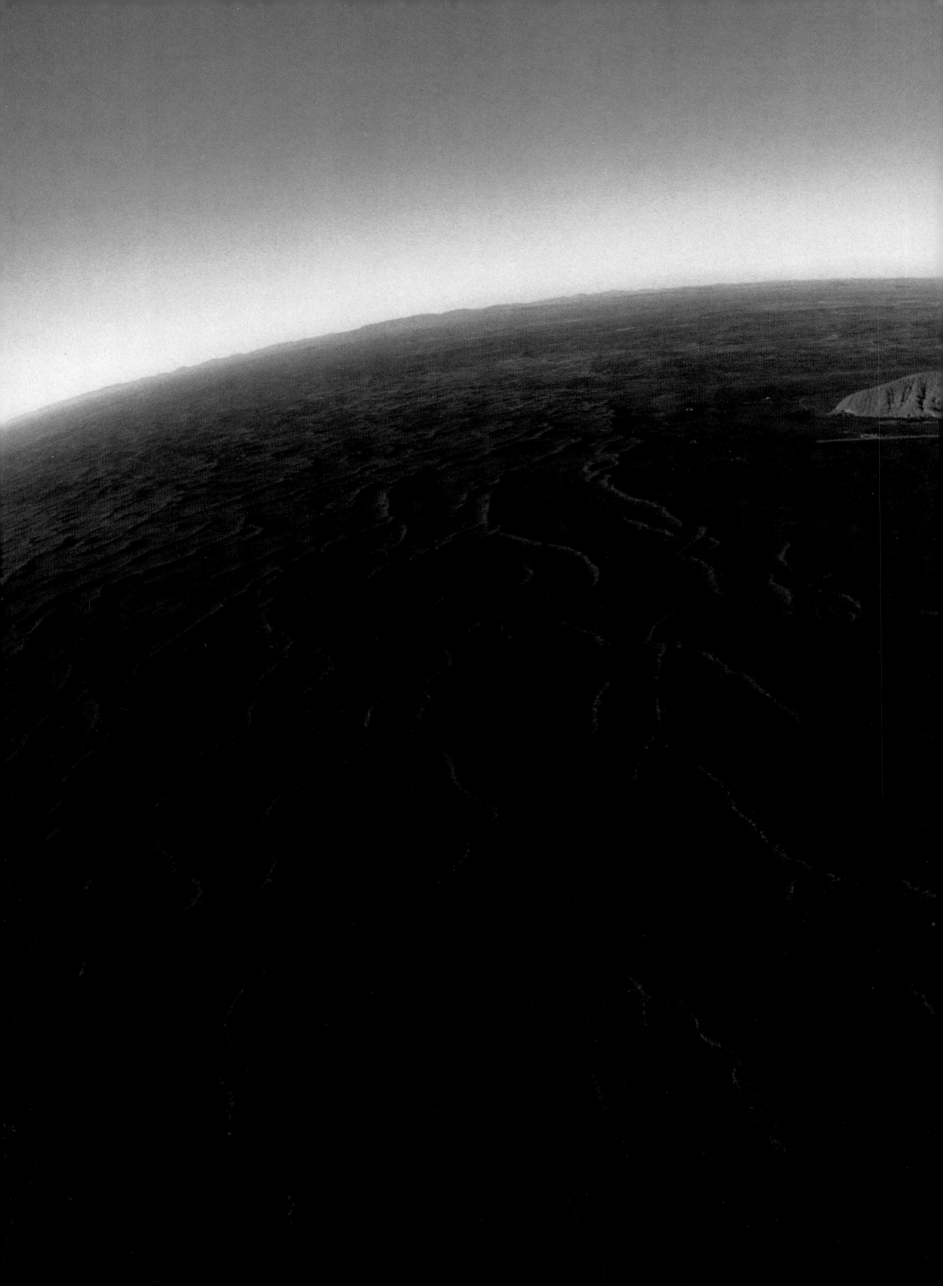

Jan Oliver-Geke and daughter Sally,
Paradise Valley commune, Nimbin,
New South Wales

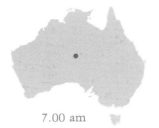

7.00 am

ETHAN HOFFMAN

Australia wakes up on a typical Friday. With a mighty stretch, camel hunter Terry Maloney, one of 15 million Australians, prepares to face the early desert chill. He will spend the day catching wild camels for export to the Middle East.

It is already 7.30 am in the eastern states and breakfast is on the stove, while four thousand kms across the continent, the west coast is still in darkness and most people have another few hours to sleep.

DAN DRY

On Carisbrooke Station, a 40,000 hectare property near Winton, Queensland, grazier Charlie Phillott, his wife Anne and daughter Helen have breakfast together before Charlie flies out to Birdsville.

Thirteen hundred km south-east of Winton, in Cowra, New South Wales, newsagent Don Kibbler starts his morning deliveries.

A few blocks away, Cowra postie Ron Jeffs delivers Bill Langfield's mail.

21

PIERRE BOULAT

'A wall of water. All that water with the dry country stretching away.' In Kununurra, Western Australia, French photographer Pierre Boulat was surprised to find two men fishing in the dam before they went to work.

Left
Converted workers cottages in fashionable Paddington, Sydney, were originally built between 1850 and 1900 as workers' cottages, and have been renovated to provide convenient inner suburban living.

PATRICK WARD

Flinders Street Station, Melbourne,
Victoria

Right
On holiday in the Northern Territory,
Japanese tourist Tsutomu Onodera
begins the final day of his week-long
desert tour from Alice Springs to
Ayers Rock.

Far right
Approach to the Sydney Harbour
Bridge

CARY WOLINSKY

STEPHANIE MAZE

PHIL HUBER

Melbourne Grammar student, Park Street, Melbourne

Left
Bathurst Island, Northern Territory

Right
Celeste Geer, Tina McGlaughlin and 'Toffee' wait for a tram *en route* to Lauriston Girls School in the Melbourne suburb of Armadale.

PHILLIP JONES GRIFFITHS

DAVID HARVEY

Schoolchildren at the Lombardina
Mission, Western Australia. The
nearest city is Port Hedland, over
600 km to the south. The mission is
surrounded by hundreds of kilometres
of beach and bush.

Left
On Ann Street in Brisbane, Queensland, a punter listens to the scratch-
ings for the next race meeting.

Far left
At South Australia's Lindsay Park
Stud farm, famous for its thorough-
bred race horses, Kerrie Mariani gives
her daughter Kristie her morning bath.

DONNA FERRATO

Fourth generation baker, John
Cadzow, Miles, Queensland

NICOLE BENGIVENO

Bill Nugent has been the baker in
Nimbin, New South Wales, for seven
years. His daily output is 1,800 loaves
all baked in a wood-fired brick oven.

JOHN LAMB

Neville Richards, Korumburra,
Victoria

31

9.00 am

The photographs on this page, the previous two pages and the following two pages were all taken at exactly 9 am. Each of the 100 photographers had been instructed to photograph a small business proprietor in front of their establishment.

Previous page

Bendigo, Victoria

34

1	2	3
4	5	6
7	8	9

1 Melbourne, Victoria

2 Mullumbimby, NSW

3 Melbourne, Victoria

4 Melbourne, Victoria

5 Kangaroo Island, SA

6 Perth, Western Australia

7 Geelong, Victoria

8 Bright, Victoria

9 Ballarat, Victoria

Kalgoorlie, Western Australia

The two domestic airlines in Australia carry approximately 26,000 passengers each day. Australians travel by air a great deal because long distances between capital cities make driving and even train travel too slow. New passenger terminals at Kingsford Smith Airport in Sydney *(right)* have been remodelled to accommodate this advancing industry.

ARNAUD DE WILDENBERG

Irrigation by giant sprinklers is a common sight along the Murray River near Mildura, Victoria. Australia is the driest continent on Earth, and although the technology exists for widespread irrigation, the water itself is too often unavailable for larger schemes to be worthwhile.

Left
Dairy farmer Wal Dowell of
Korumburra in south-eastern Victoria
spends a tranquil hour moving his
Jerseys into a new paddock. He'll be
out again in the late afternoon to
drive the cattle in for milking.

Below
As part of a school project, 10-year-old
David Wintle brought 11-year-old
'Kohine' to the Korumburra Primary
School. The project was a great
success and, with the help of Daniel
Doull, was concluded with the oldest
dairying stunt known to man.

Below
The morning is full of responsibility
for 'Warragul', a Queensland
champion Blue Heeler. Heelers are
renowned for their ability to control
cattle—a nip on the heel and a steer is
on its way. The Brahman bull is
headed for Indonesia as breeding stock.

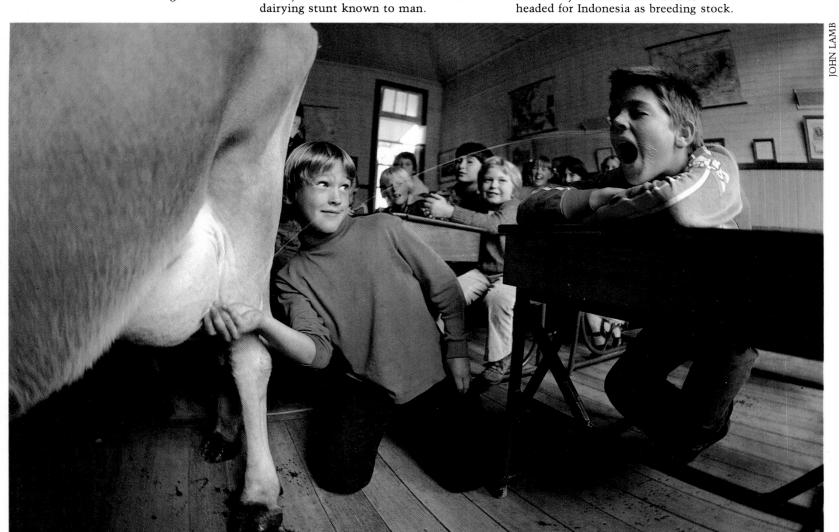

JOHN LAMB

DAN BUDNICK

ARTHUR GRACE

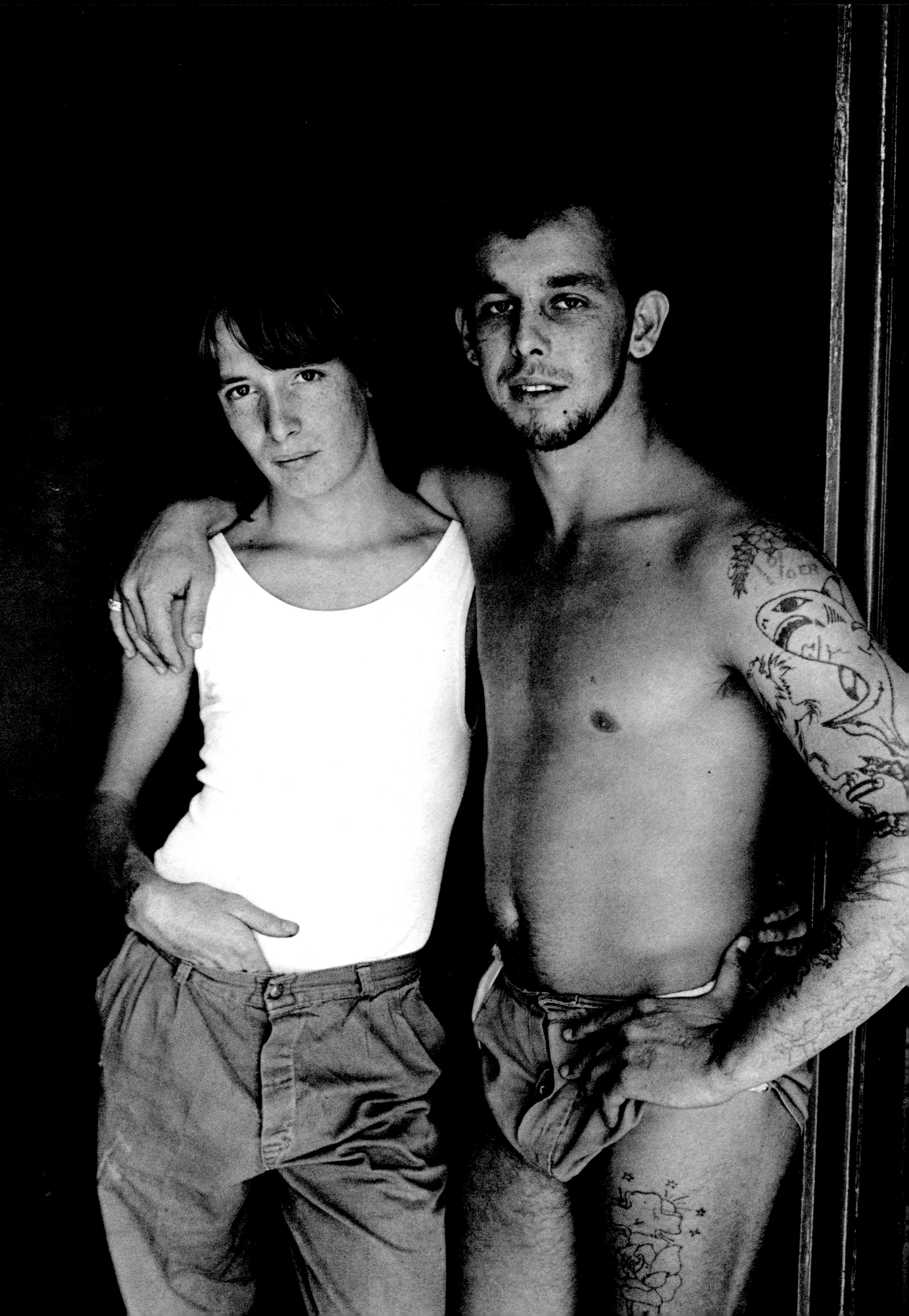

ARTHUR GRACE

ALMOST 10,000 Australians were in prison on Friday, March 6. American photographer Arthur Grace spent the day inside the walls of the Adelaide Gaol in South Australia. He was the first foreign photojournalist ever given complete freedom to photograph inside an Australian prison. *'I had a chance to speak with a number of the prisoners, many of whom asked me to photograph them. There were two basic complaints. The first was that the prison (built in 1839) was antiquated—they use buckets instead of toilets. To be locked inside a cell with that for 14 hours every night is inhuman—the cells are tiny little holes.'*

The day began at 8 am when cell doors were opened. Grace's first photographs were of waste buckets being emptied. Later in the day, in the presence of a prison officer, a new inmate took a shower as part of the admission procedure.

'The prisoners' other major complaint was the snail's pace of the judicial system. The prisoners awaiting trial just never know when they are going to get to court. They sit there in those little holes waiting and waiting.'

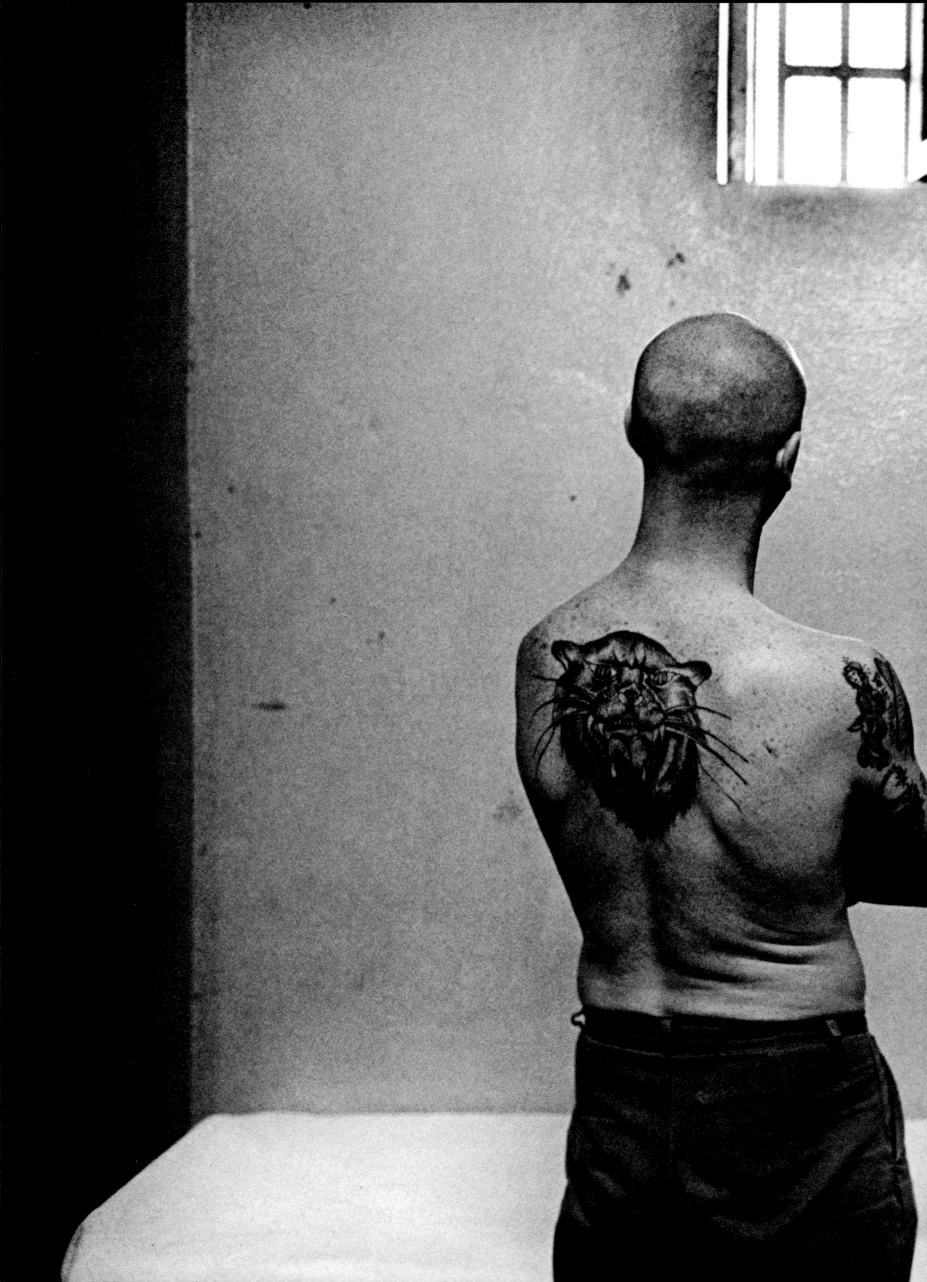

High Court Judges, Canberra

9.30 am

Ayers Rock (Uluru), Northern Territory

Ayers Rock and, in the background, the Olgas have recently become major tourist attractions in central Australia. In 1981, the Rock was climbed by more than 250,000 people. In the face of such booming tourism, local aboriginal tribes continue their age-old ceremonies involving 'Uluru' (meaning 'sacred and permanent') in a small reserve at the northern end of the monolith. To them, Uluru symbolises oneness with nature and is the gravitational centre of the continent.

53

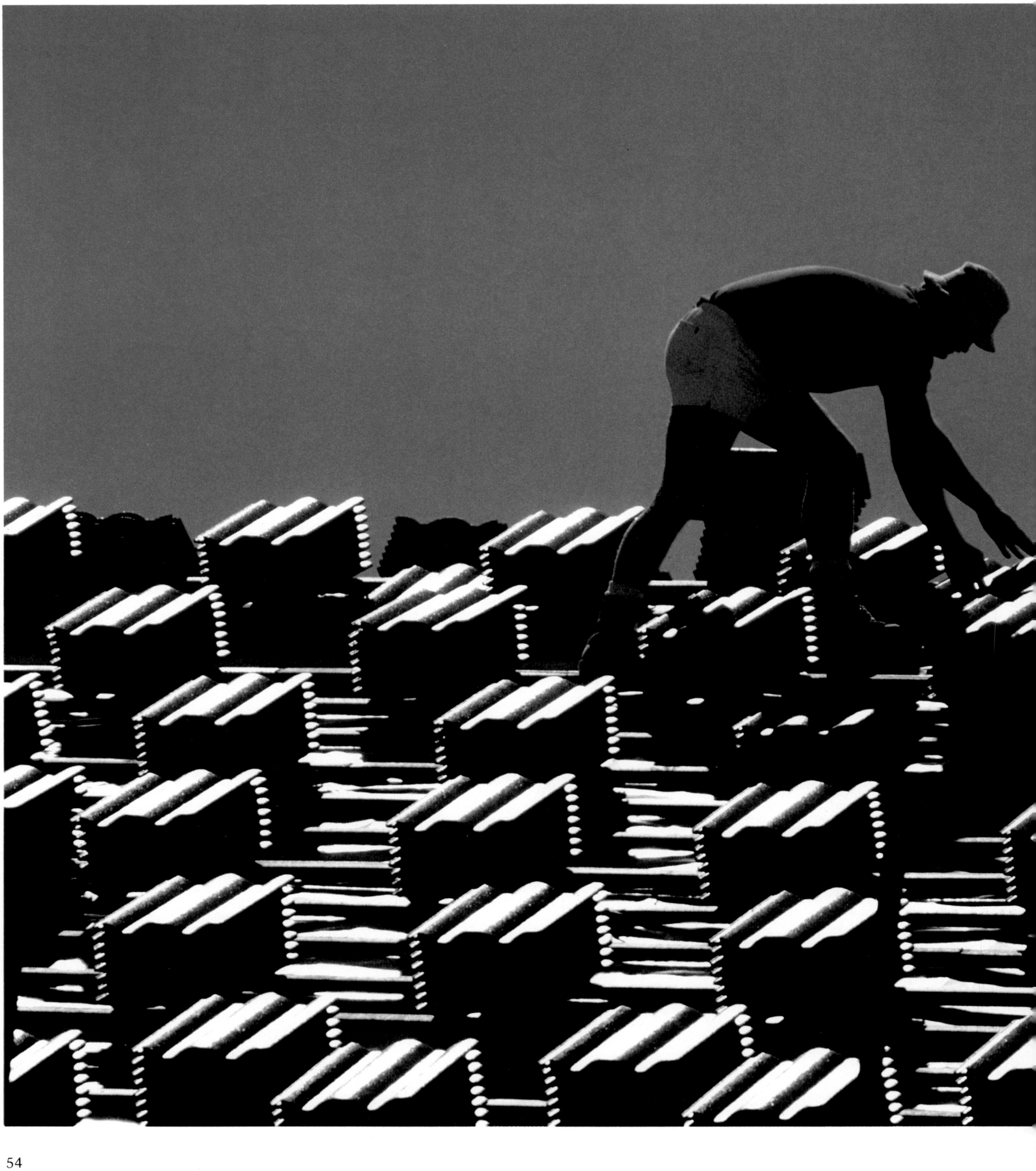

BRUCE POSTLE

With the day's work stacked around him, Morry Kite makes a last minute check of his tiles before laying them on the roof of the Mirinjani Retirement Village in Weston, a Canberra suburb.

Redfern, Sydney

Above
Steve Dennis, twice Australian champion, trains at the Roy Carroll Gym in Chippendale, a Sydney suburb. Dennis keeps his fighting weight at 66.5 kg with a series of twelve workouts of 3 minutes each. In addition to the normal regimen of sparring, skip rope and punching bags, he runs 10–12 kilometres every night. A week after this photograph was taken, Dennis defeated Gary Stevens, the eighth world-ranked welterweight.

Above
In a training room in the Roy Carroll Gym are Trevor Christian *(in steam box)*, the only aboriginal boxing referee; Mickey Fernandez, Dennis' manager; trainer John Lewis *(second from left)*; and assistant Jack Bell. The Roy Carroll Gym has been a centre for aboriginal boxers since 1963.

Carroll, an aboriginal ex-Riverina middleweight champ, promotes professional sports because they provide jobs for his people. It's a sad comment that sports are one of the few areas where young aboriginals are judged solely on ability.

Following page
The 'Bridge People' live under Townsville's Victoria Bridge.

10.00 am

Antique jewellery at Kozminsky
Galleries captivates a shopping duo on
Bourke Street in Melbourne.

Kununurra, Western Australia,

Morning shopper outside Perth's
Central Railway Station

10.30 am

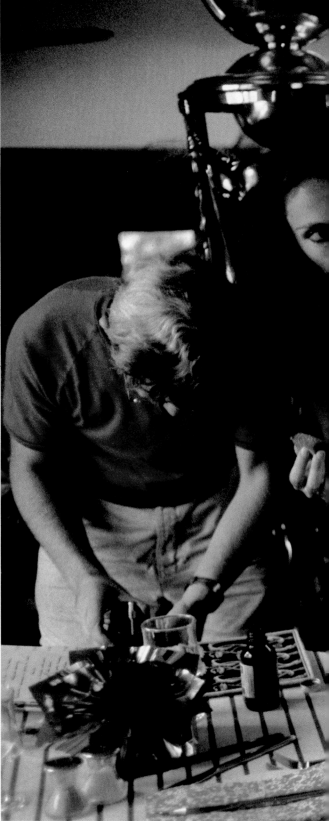

Photographer Bill Pierce, whose reportage has covered the North American and European film industries, spent the day on the set of ''Heatwave'' in Sydney. *It doesn't look like the American film industry. You ask yourself why all these people are standing around with a Panaflex camera in some guy's living room. The cameraman moves a prop when the prop man is busy, and the director might move a light. Crews and budgets are smaller. The films are simple and straight forward. They take a single, executable script and put time and effort into that—they don't waste time and effort on nonsense.*

Judy Davis is **the** *woman in Australian film as far as the public is concerned. She's very good, definitely headed for celebrity status, but she says she's an actress, not a star. The story here is people in film, not the film industry.'*

Left and below
'Heatwave' director Phil Noyce ('Newsfront') and star Judy Davis ('My Brilliant Career') on location in a suburban, working class home in South Sydney.

10.30 am

STAN FORMAN

Sydney

Sydney

10.30 am

Left
On Cosy Corner beach near Albany in Western Australia, Ken Mitchell has had a good morning. The salmon appeared off the beach just after dawn, and after a few hours they hit his nets—before 10 am the truck was almost full, ready for a trip to the nearby cannery. With luck he will be back on the beach and have his nets re-set before the fish appear again in the afternoon.

Following page
At the age of 32, Mrs. Huriye Furuncu left Turkey and migrated with her family to Melbourne. For the past eight years she has been working in Brunswick clothing factories. Every harvest season, despite the long hours and low wages, she and three of her seven children go north to Shepparton to pick fruit and vegetables. Mrs. Furuncu says she still hopes to return to Turkey someday.

SUSAN MEISELAS

JACK CORN

Far left and Following page
Shepparton Preserving Company,
Victoria.

Left
Puck's Room, Kangaroo Lake, near
Swan Hill.

TERRY STRAIGHT

Tara, Queensland

Mt Isa Queensland

73

DIRCK HALSTEAD

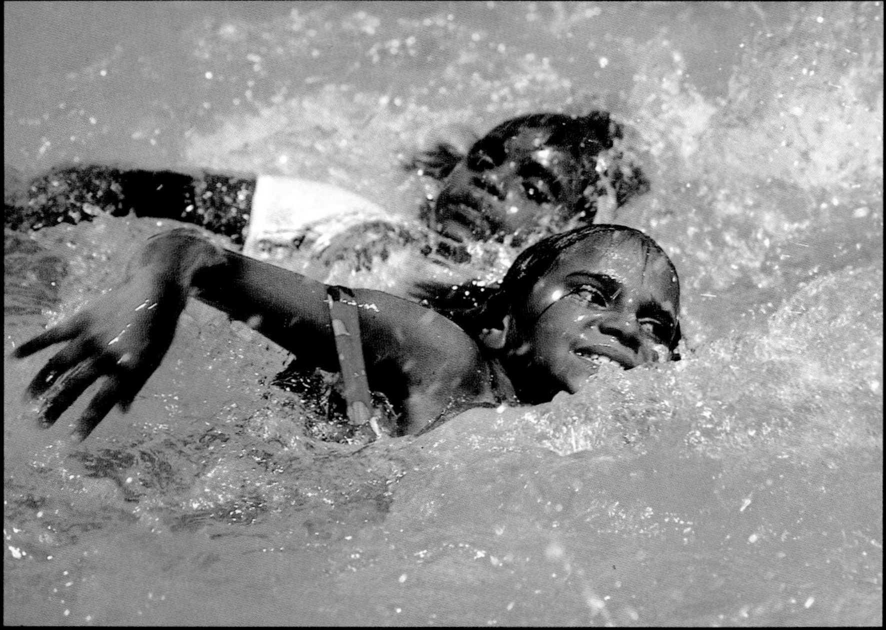

NICOLE BENGIVENO

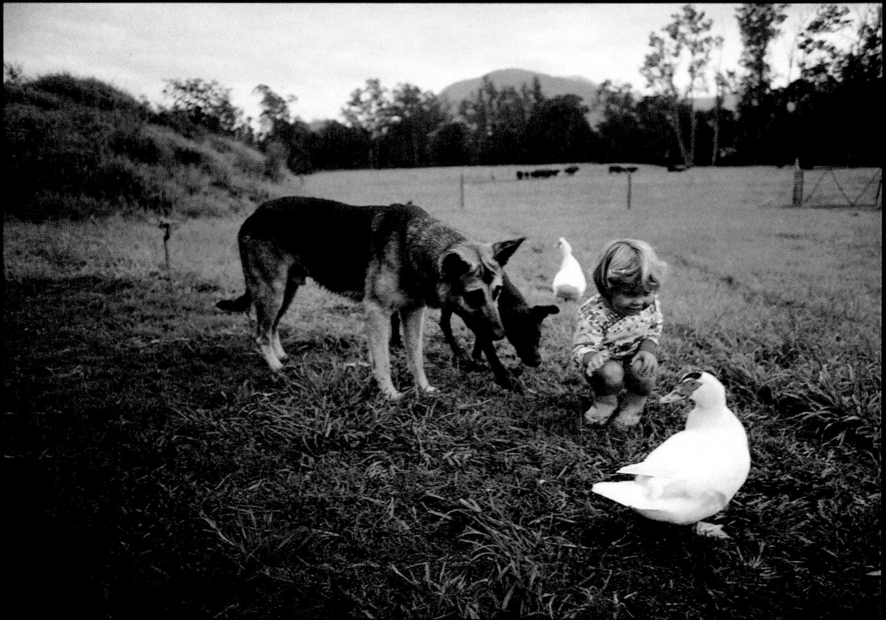

BRUCE POSTLE

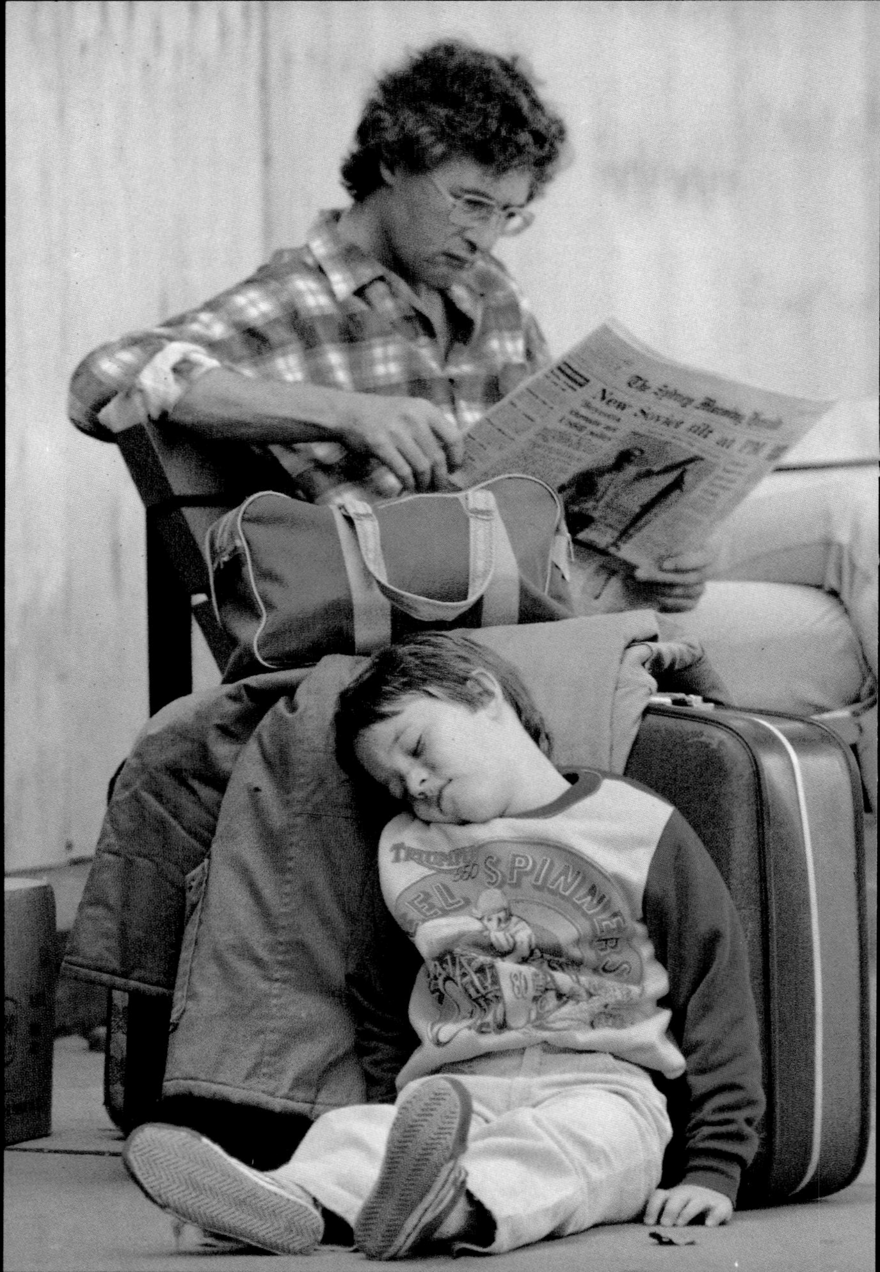

11.00 am

Burketown, Queensland

Perth

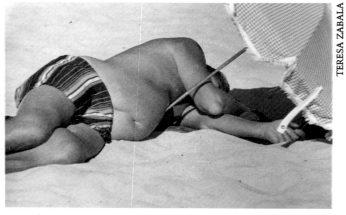

Not everyone worked on Friday, and with a day off, the beach is the best place to polish the suntan. Unfortunately, this exposure to the Australian summer sun gives Australians the highest rate of skin cancer in the world.

11:30 am

Above
In Western Australia, Swiss photographer Rene Burri was fascinated by the relationship between Telecom Australia and the Perth surfing community.

HAN JUCE

NICOLE BENGIVENO

The Hare Krishna farm, at Murwillumbah in north-eastern New South Wales is a place for meditation, celebrations and festivals. Gopi (*right*) has entered the diety chamber where offerings are made to Krishna. Avatari, her daughter Ambika, and friends (*above*) are in the communal dining area where farm produce constitutes the daily fare and makes this 10-year-old settlement virtually self-sufficient.

INDIAN photographer Dilip Mehta has photographed religious ceremonies and festivals all over the world. When he arrived in Australia he had just finished shooting a religious festival in India and was overwhelmed by the contrast in lifestyles. *'To go directly from seeing people starving in India to a society that has a surplus of everything just stunned me.'* Mehta flew to Western Australia for his assignment on March 6—to photograph the Benedictine Monks at New Norcia, 140 km north of Perth. Established in 1846 by Spanish Benedictines exiled from their homeland, these early religious settlers set up a mission to minister to the natives. The Spanish influence on the area remains—olive groves, bell towers, stucco walls, and many of the customs within the mission. Mehta's initial reaction to the town was hesitant. *'I drove into town and before I knew it there was a sign saying "Thank you for visiting New Norcia." It was one of those photographers' nightmares where you say to yourself, "My God, there's nothing here to photograph!" I was really nervous and asked the first monk I met, Father Justin, if it would* be OK to smoke. *He laughed and told me he was a chain smoker himself. He said the other monks had nick-named him 'Father Filter'. Once I began to feel welcome at the monastary, I realised what a contrast it was to the religious festival I'd just come from in India. There the festivities had been noisy, garish, and frantic. Here I was, a week later, surrounded by an unbelievable calmness and serenity. It was that serenity that I decided I wanted to portray in my photographs.'*

DILIP MEHTA

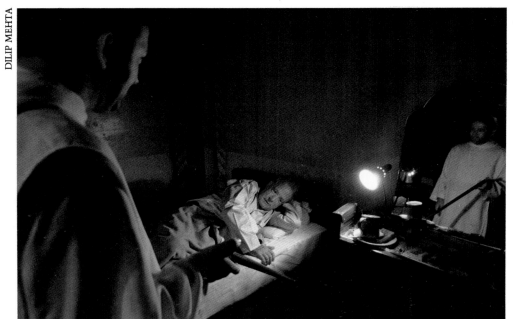

Far left
Some of the younger monks (in civilian clothes) have planned a retreat into the bush and Father Justin gives them his blessing before their departure.

Left
Inside the monastery Dom Francis visits Abbot Gregory who has injured his back and is spending the day in bed resting.

Below
Novitiate monks spend several hours each week studying in the monastery library. Some earn teaching certification and instruct at Salvado College, while others learn a trade and help run the monastery or its associated cottage industries.

Right
The monks' vow of poverty is very much in evidence. They have very few possessions. Dom Francis has one set of work clothes, one winter habit, and two summer habits, and his room is a model of practical efficiency.

Below
The religious curriculum is the subject of this Salvado College faculty meeting. The College, named after Mission founder Dom Rosendo Salvado, was amalgamated from existing mission schools in 1974. It now provides co-educational boarding facilities for 200 high school students.

Dom Francis (above) and Dom Christopher (below).

The role of the missionary in outback Australia has been both lavishly praised and bitterly condemned. Nineteenth century missionaries brought the aboriginal people their first experience of western religion and often of western medicine as well. But the new faith brought a new culture, complete with previously unknown diseases (especially leprosy, heart disease and alcoholism). Within 100 years traditional aboriginal life had disappeared and much of the aboriginal culture lay in ruin. The problems continue today— trachoma (a chronic eye disease which can result in blindness) affects one in three aboriginal children in the outback, the aboriginal infant mortality rate is four times the national average, and the life expectancy for an aboriginal is 25 years less than that of a white Australian.

MIKE O'BRIEN

Patrol Padre Don Kube *(right)* flies his Cessna into some of the remotest settlements in Western Australia. He performs baptisms, weddings and funerals for 500 individuals located on 140 sheep and cattle stations spread over 400,000 km ^{2}. Although officially attached to the Uniting Church, the Patrol Padres can't afford the luxury of denomination—with such enormous areas to cover, the Churches work together to minister to these very isolated people. Padre Don leads the funeral service for the late Diamond White. Friends and relatives *(above)* mourn the deceased, one of Meekatharras best known stockmen. On March 6, across Australia, 297 other families are also in mourning.

MIKE O'BRIEN

Right
Raymond Kantilla, of the Tiwi people on Bathurst Island (north of Darwin) is ready to dance in the Kulama ceremony, remembering the spirits of Tribal Ancestors.

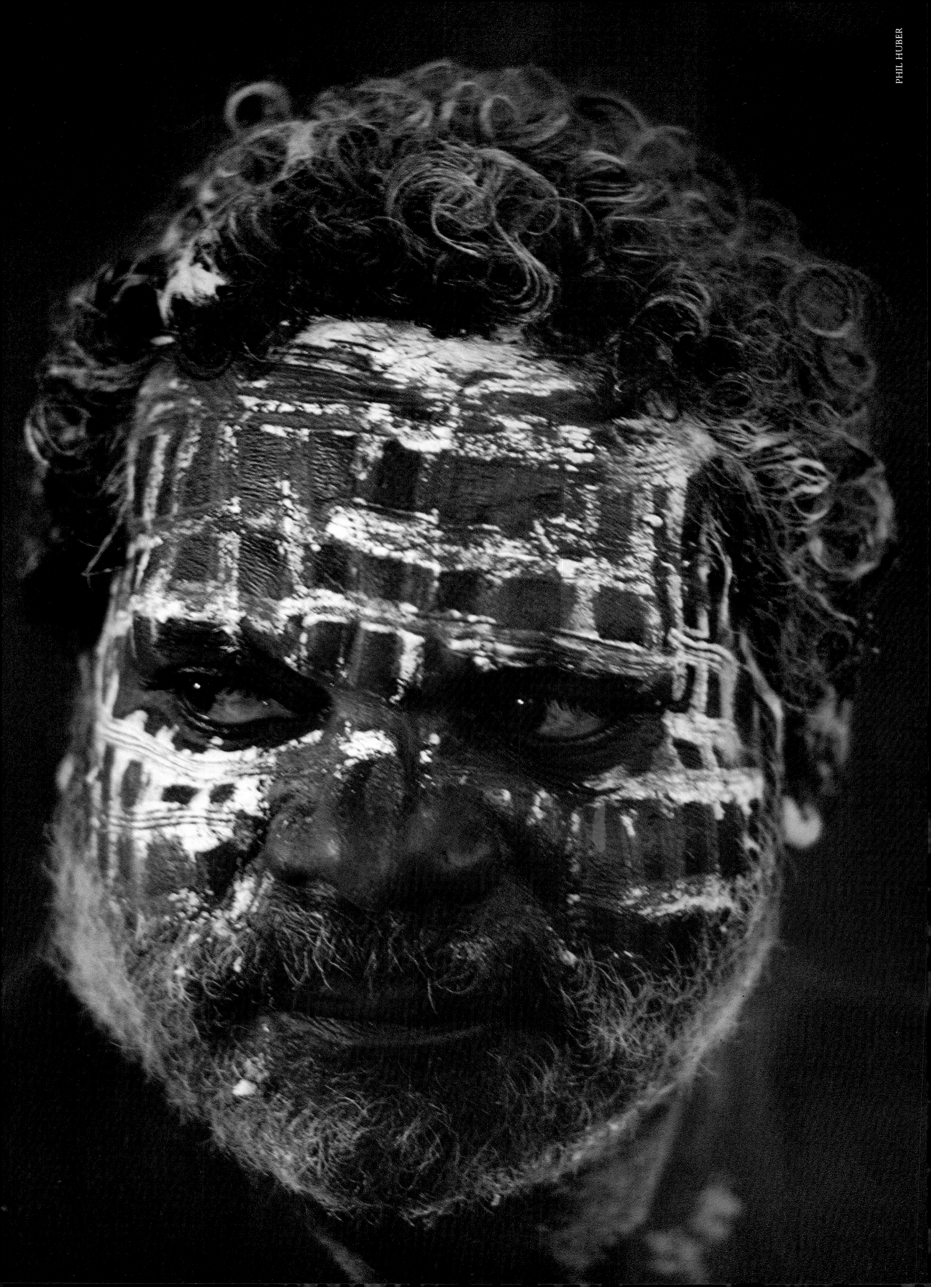

Beagle Bay, Western Australia.

KENT KOBERSTEEN

(Above)

Students at Yirara College in Alice Springs practice Yoga in class. One of two colleges for aboriginals in the Northern Territory, Yirara attempts a bi-cultural education for its students. The curriculum includes: Tribal languages, English, mathematics, science, comparative cultures, and several courses designed to encourage creative living while unemployed.

Unemployment is a situation many aboriginals are familiar with, as an estimated 65 percent of the aboriginal workforce is unemployed nationwide. While most schools teach students with the idea that they will eventually join the workforce, Yirara must cope with the fact that most of its students will never have full time jobs.

Young boy from Bathurst Island,
with his pet carpet snake.

The recess marble game at
Collingwood State School,
Melbourne.

STEPHANIE MAZE

Following pages
Left
In the Northern Territory, workers ride with a shipment of uranium oxide (yellow cake) on board a chartered plane from Nabarlek to Darwin.

Right
Reg Feeny of Coorabulla Station is having a tooth pulled by flying doctor Clive Allardyce. Dr Allardyce flew to the station to treat Reg and check on two other patients, and will soon leave to continue his rounds which may cover 1200 km per day.

HIROJI KUBOTA

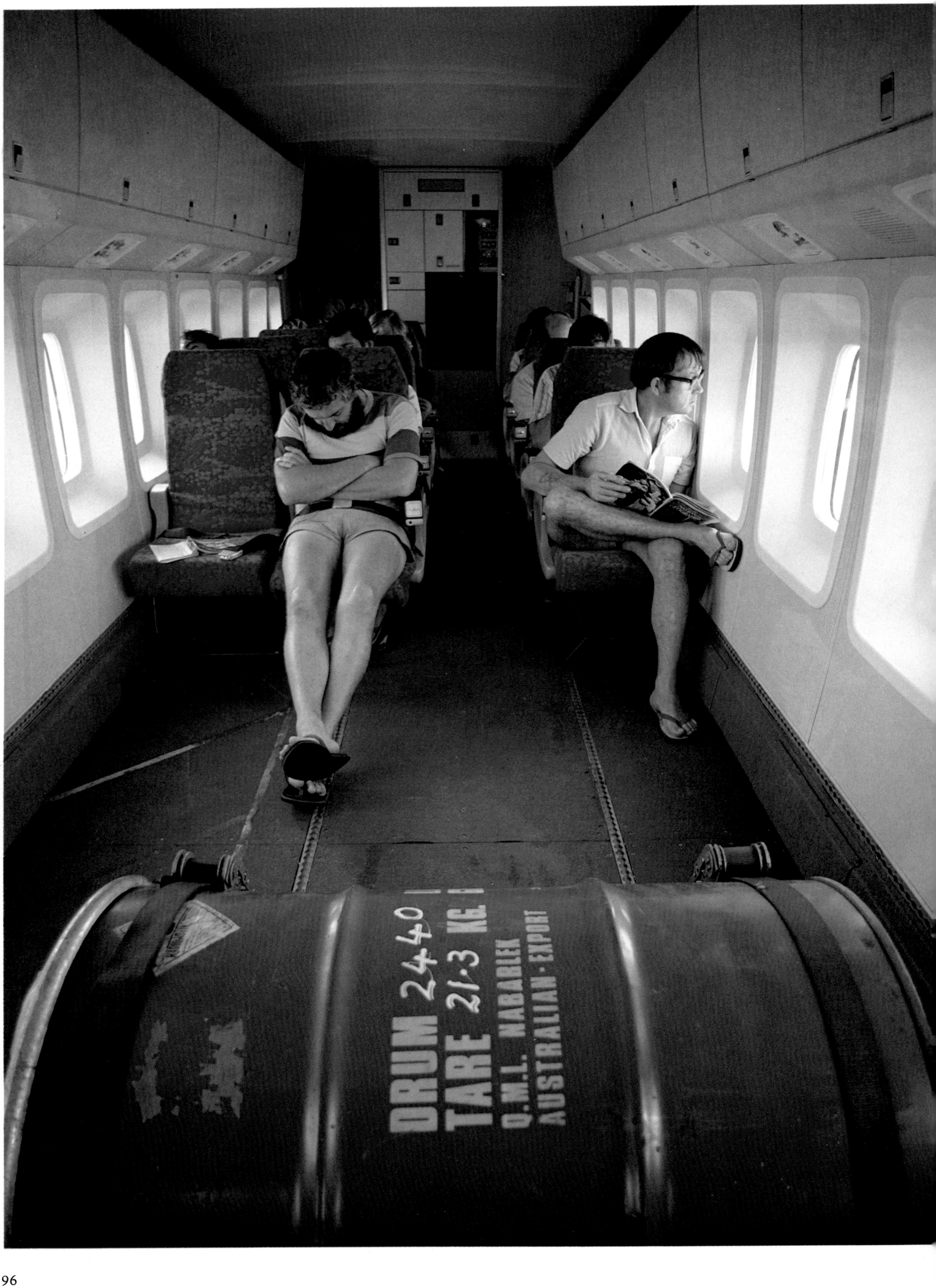

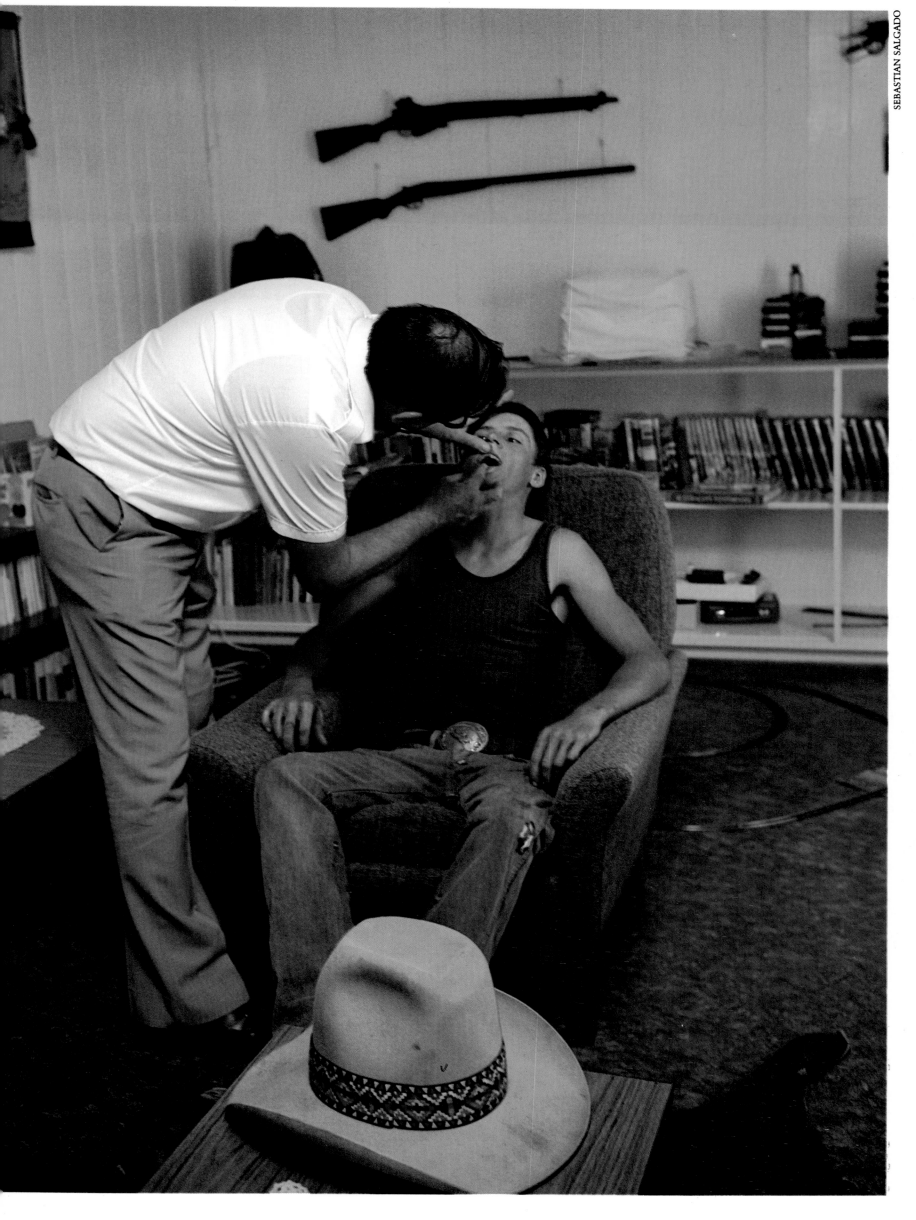

DAVID BURNETT

NICOLE BENGIVENO

KENT KOBERSTEEN

GREGORY HEISLER

Trackwalker John Garbutt, repairing track, Western Australia

Arnhem Land, Northern Territory

2.00 pm

Famous in part for its changes in colour during the day, Uluru is nearly as internationally well-known as the Sydney Opera House. Climbing 348 metres above the surrounding plain, it has been a major element in aboriginal Dreamtime legends for thousands of years. Explorer Ernest Giles dubbed it Ayers Rock in 1872, to honour the incumbent governor of South Australia, Sir Henry Ayers.

104

Steel Works, Whyalla, South Australia

Shepparton Preserving Company,
Victoria

Josephine Adarve, woollen spinner

The Albany Woollen Mills specialises in spinning and dyeing carpet yarns. The mill is one of the largest employers in the City of Albany, operating 24 hours a day. The women on these pages are beginning the evening shift.

DIEGO GOLDBERG

Woollen winder Debbie Wals wears a watch-like 'wrist applicator' which dispenses latex to join the ends of yarn together as scoured wool is spun onto tubes.

Rita Abrahams, woollen spinner

Jenny McCarthy, woollen winder

Tanunda, South Australia

HARRY MATTISON

STEVE KRONGARD

DAVID ALAN HARVEY

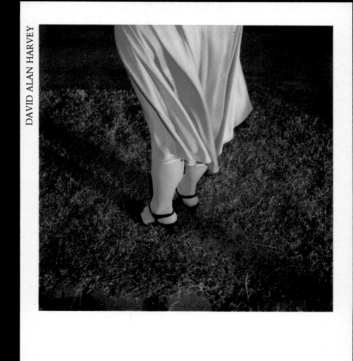

DAVID ALAN HARVEY

Polaroid Australia supplied 'A Day in the Life of Australia' photographers with SX-70 film and cameras to use during the project.
The images above and those on pages 206–207 are selected from photographs that were shot on Friday, March 6.

Cowra, New South Wales

2.30 pm

HERVE GLOAGUEN

Above
When asked if he had lived in the
Northern Territory all his life,
Urapunga stockman Chris Fryer
replied, *'Not yet'*.

Left
Longreach, Queensland

SUSAN McELHINNEY

Above
Auction, Ballarat, Victoria

Right
Country show, Tara, Queensland

Mooroopna Primary School, Shepparton

Olympic Pool, Mt. Isa
Queensland

JANE ATWOOD

Jamie Kir

AMERICAN photographer Jane Atwood began photographing blind children in Paris three years ago. In 1980, she won the first W. Eugene Smith Memorial Grant for Humanistic Photography, enabling her to continue her work. On March 6, her assignment was to photograph children at the Royal Victorian Institute for the Blind in Melbourne. *'What strikes you first when you spend time with blind children is that most of the young ones don't realise they are blind—they are children first and blind second. Their attitude about what it means to be blind comes from* *their parents. You see so many blind adults who are awkward and embarrassed about their blindness—as if they were guilty of something. If their parents love them and accept their blindness, the children have a good opinion of themselves. In Australia there is a very positive attitude between teachers, parents, and children. When mothers see other mothers facing the same problems it makes it easier for all of them. The Institute has a wonderful programme where retired people come at night and read to the children, and then put them to bed. It's sort of homey.*

Kristian Kupc

Mary Roche

Kelly Jordan

Right
Children enjoy the Water Tunnel at
Melbourne's annual Moomba Festiva

134

3.00 pm

COLIN BEARD

GARY CHAPMAN

Above
Crooked River, Victoria

Left
Katherine, Northern Territory

Arnhem Land, Northern Territory

137

PASCALE HASTINGS   age 8

VICTORIA YOUNG   age 9

ANDREW HOPKINS   age 16

JONATHAN KRAGER   age 7

SCOTT MACKENZIE   age 10

ANNIE PALEY   age 12

138

JONATHAN KRAGER age

FIONA SMITH age 12

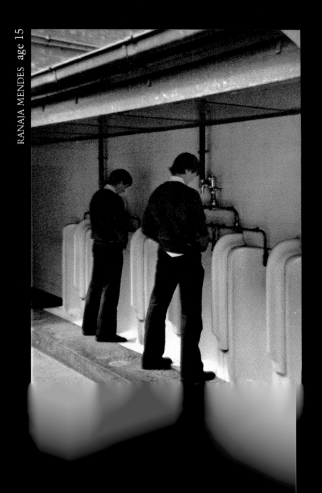
RANAJA MENDES age 15

GRANT CHESTERFIELD age 13

`Kodak (Australasia) distributed 200

Above
Kalgoorlie, Western Australia

Left
The Prime Minister spent Friday morning at his home in Nareen, Victoria, in the company of family, friends, and 'Bert' (left). As a photographer participating in *A Day in the Life of Australia,* Mr. Fraser Shot photographs around Nareen in the morning and then flew to Canberra to attend the funeral of Senator John Knight.

Western Australia.

Prize Santa Gertrudis bulls at the
Boorowa Show in southern New
South Wales.

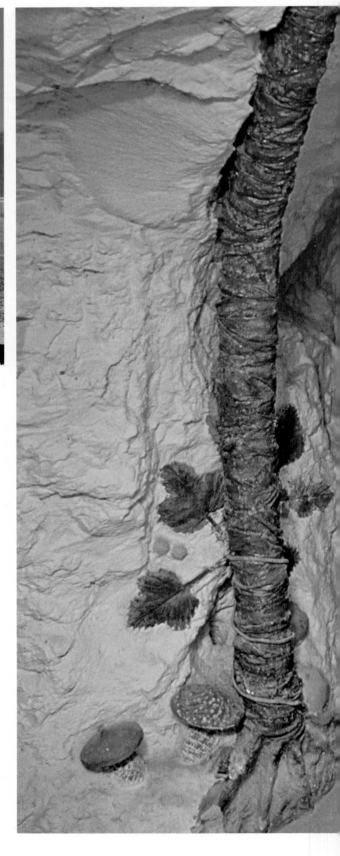

DIRCK HALSTEAD

Opal miner, artist, sculptor, and entrepreneur 'Crocodile' Harry and his wife Marta stand in the entrance to their underground home in Coober Pedy, South Australia. Harry is a German baron who came to Australia after the Second World War. He spent many years in the North as a crocodile hunter, then moved to Coober Pedy to try his hand at opal mining. Marta, also an artist, first read about Harry in a magazine in Germany. She was fascinated by his story, wrote to him, and they began corresponding. After a vivid dream where she saw Harry seriously injured, Marta left Germany and came to Australia to be with Harry. They now divide their time between mining, art, and the tourist industry.

Perth

Melbourne

Rockhampton, Queensland

Artist Brett Whitely at work on his
latest painting 'just like a woman,
Bondi 1981' in Sydney

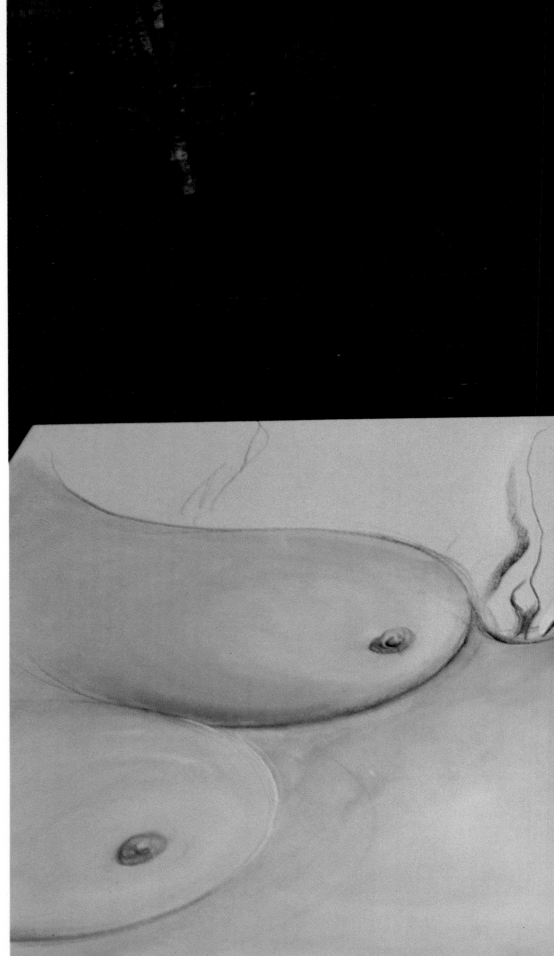

St. Kilda Road, Melbourne

East Malvern, Victoria

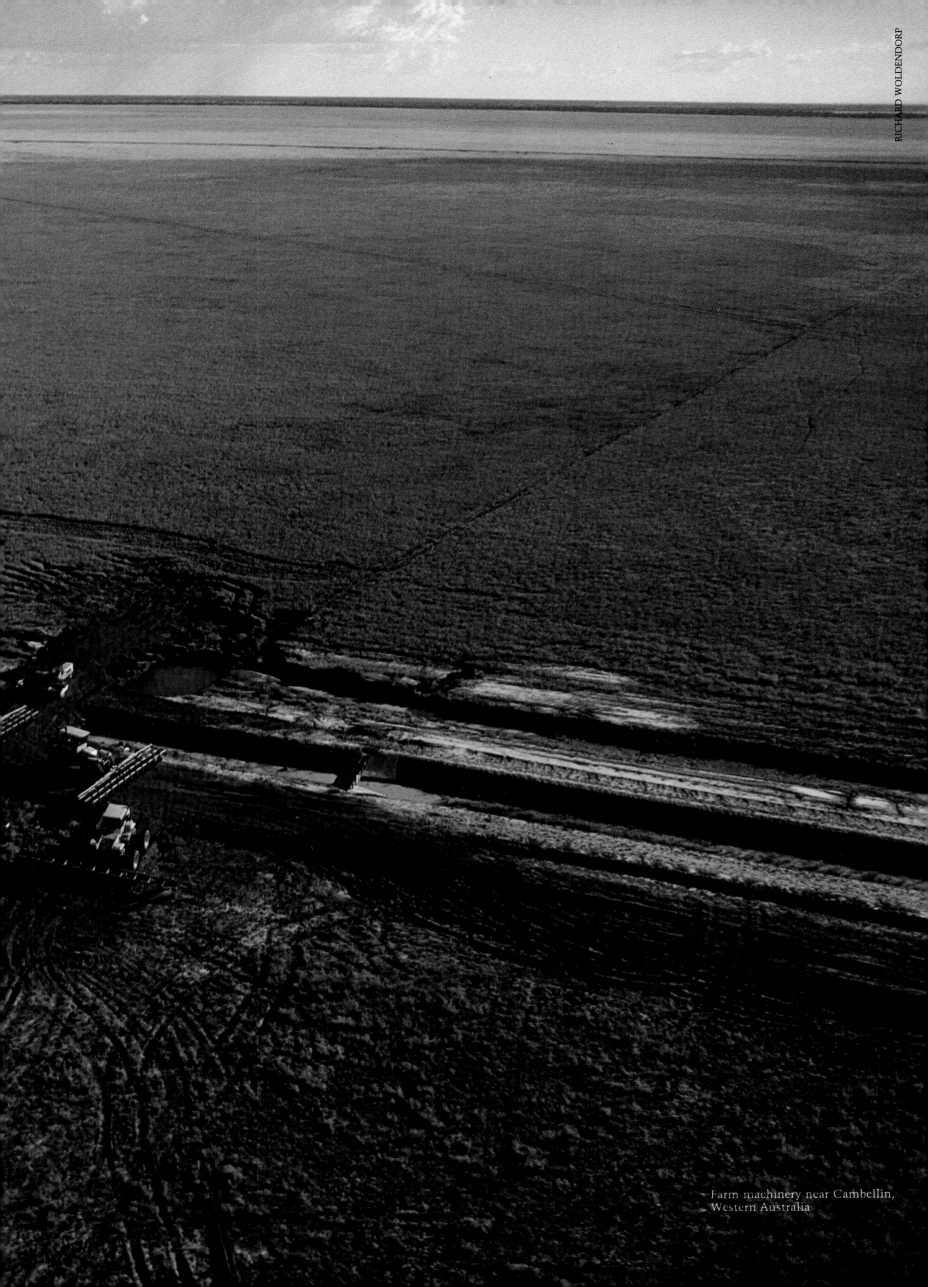

Farm machinery near Cambellin,
Western Australia

Parndana Bowling Club, Kangaroo
Island, South Australia

The Gap Youth Centre, Alice Springs

Australian photographer John Marmaras grew up in the 1950s as part of the Greek community in Melbourne—the third largest Greek community in the world. After working overseas for the past seventeen years he returned to participate in *A Day in the Life of Australia* project. *'It's not until you get out of a place that you really get to see what it's like.'* He observed that the pressures to conform to an anglo-saxon lifestyle had shifted focus since his childhood, the emphasis now being on the newer waves of immigrants.

On March 6, John photographed the scenes of his childhood: fish markets, cafes, clubs, a Greek community school, and a traditional Greek Orthodox funeral. John recalls being so moved by the funeral, that tears were streaming down his face behind the camera. Two weeks later he returned to the same church for another funeral—this time for a member of his own family.

Lonsdale Street, Melbourne

Left and far left
Footscray Fishmarket, Melbourne

Following page
The Orpheus Club, Russell Street, Melbourne

163

Greek Orthodox funeral service at St. Vasilios church Staley Street, Brunswick.

Far left
St. John's Greek Orthodox School, North Carlton, Melbourne

Spinifex scrub, Western Australia

ALEX WEBB

Birdsville, Queensland

DAN DRY

GERD LUDWIG

Birdsville, Queensland

Left
Australian Hotel, Cowra, New South Wales

Far left
Gold prospectors Joe and Hec, Broad Arrow Hotel, Kalgoorlie, Western Australia

Ayers Rock

American photographer Brian Lanker was assigned to cover Normanton and Bourketown in far-north Queensland. Reproduced above is one of his contact sheets (all the images are from one roll of black and white film).

ways of taking the photograph; various angles, framings, lenses, and exposures in order to achieve different effects. Photography is subjective. There is no 'one correct way' of photographing a situation. The picture

Mulgarram Outstation, Arnhem Land

Cowra, New South Wales

Melbourne

COLIN BEARD

Dawn Wooster's family has lived in the Dargo area of Victoria since the gold rush in the mid-1800s. She and her husband Kevin run a cattle property. On March 6 the Woosters joined other cattle station owners at a regional auction at Crooked River.

Left
Margaret Loy's father came from China in the 1890s. 'He went to Golden Gate, Queensland looking for gold. It was there he married my mother. She was only sixteen. My husband was on the last ship from China before Australia closed the door. He took me for my first trip to China in 1927.' She has run the general store in Normanton since 1958. Now a widow, Margaret Loy admits 'I keep very busy. I was sorry when Mr Lanker left. I wanted to cook him a sweet'n'sour but there just wasn't time.'

Pilot Boat, 'The Rip', Port Phillip
Bay, Victoria

5.00 pm

Ramingining, Arnhem Land,
Northern Territory
Right
Fitzroy River, Western Australia

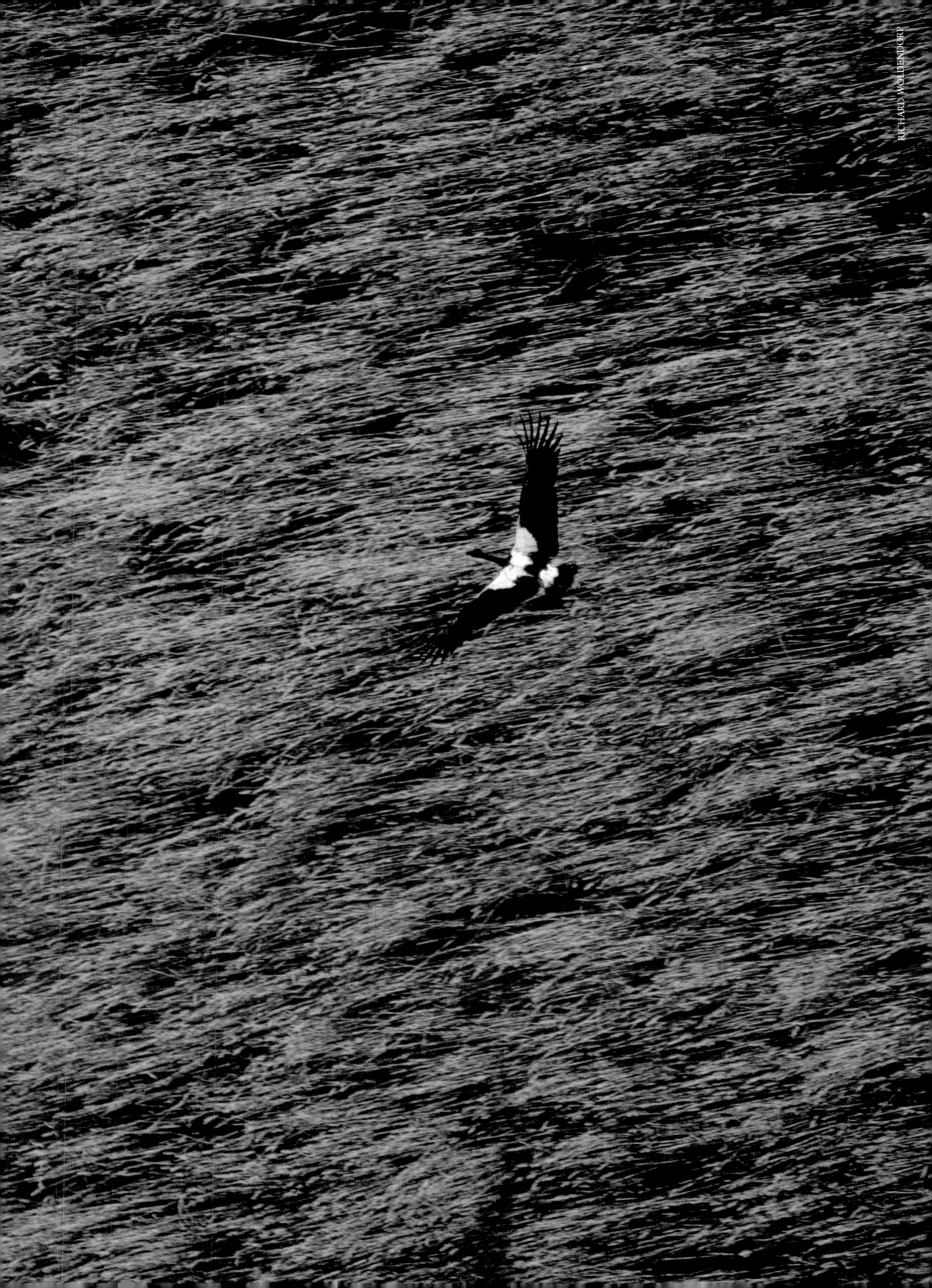

Australian photographer Carolyn Johns was particularly suited for an assignment to document the life of a district nurse in the Numurkah region of Victoria. Carolyn had spent nearly 10 years working as a nurse before establishing herself as a photographer. Her assignment on March 6 was to accompany nurse Jenny Bennie, one of the 'Blue Angels' (a term affectionately coined by the districts' elderly patients). As one of five district nurses working in the region, Jenny sees about 50 patients each week and travels within a territory of 2000 km².

Friday, like most of Jenny's days, began at dawn. At 5.30 am, before setting off for her first appointment, she helped her husband Jim milk their 90 cows and then at 7.30 am saw the children off to school. At 10 am she briefly consulted with a doctor at the Numurkah District War Memorial Hospital, before beginning her day's visits. Because of their isolation, Jenny's patients have come to depend on her not only as a nurse, but as a counsellor, confidant, and most of all, as a friend.

Mr Bert Thomas recently celebrated his 105th birthday. He lives with his daughter in Numurkah and Jenny pays him a visit at 10.30 am.

CAROLYN JOHNS

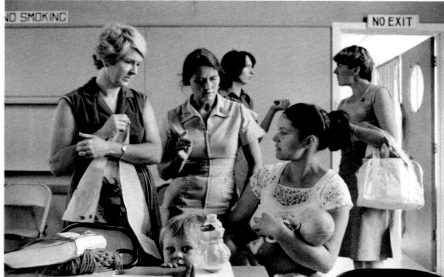

CAROLYN JOHNS

At 11 am Jenny meets with several women in the Mutual Learning Centre which also provides a creche run by several of the local unemployed girls.

District nurse Jenny Bennie

199

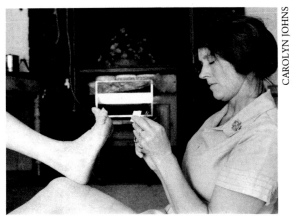

At 2.00 pm Jenny helps a patient with a pedicure.

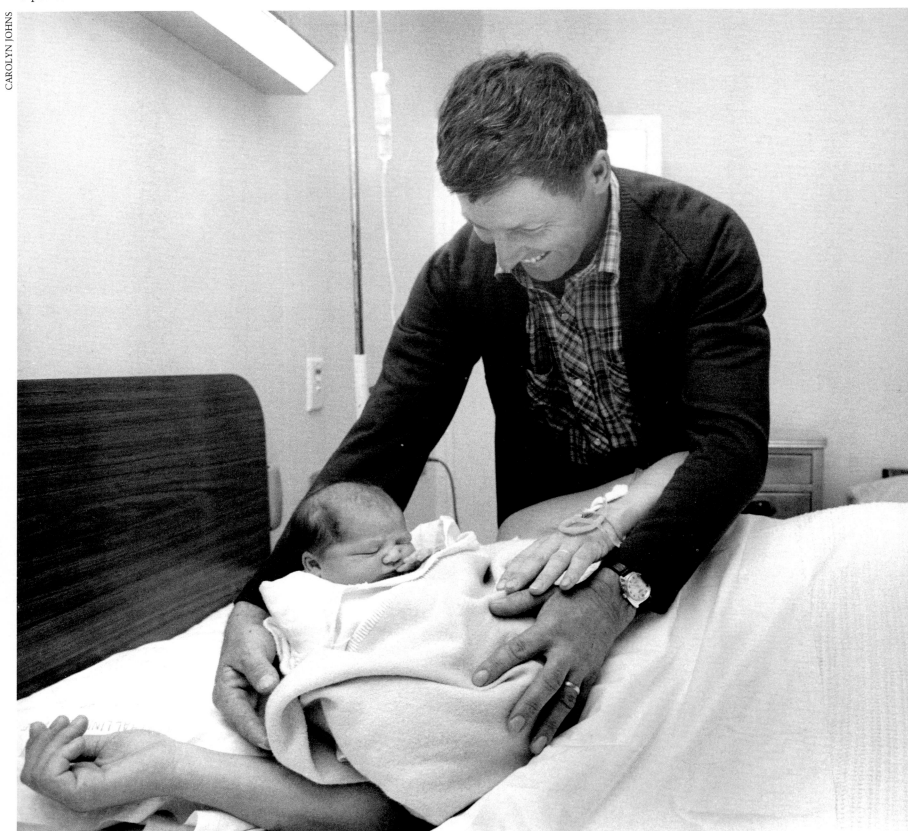

Jenny finishes her day back at the hospital and stops by to congratulate Ian and Bev Patrick on the birth of their son.

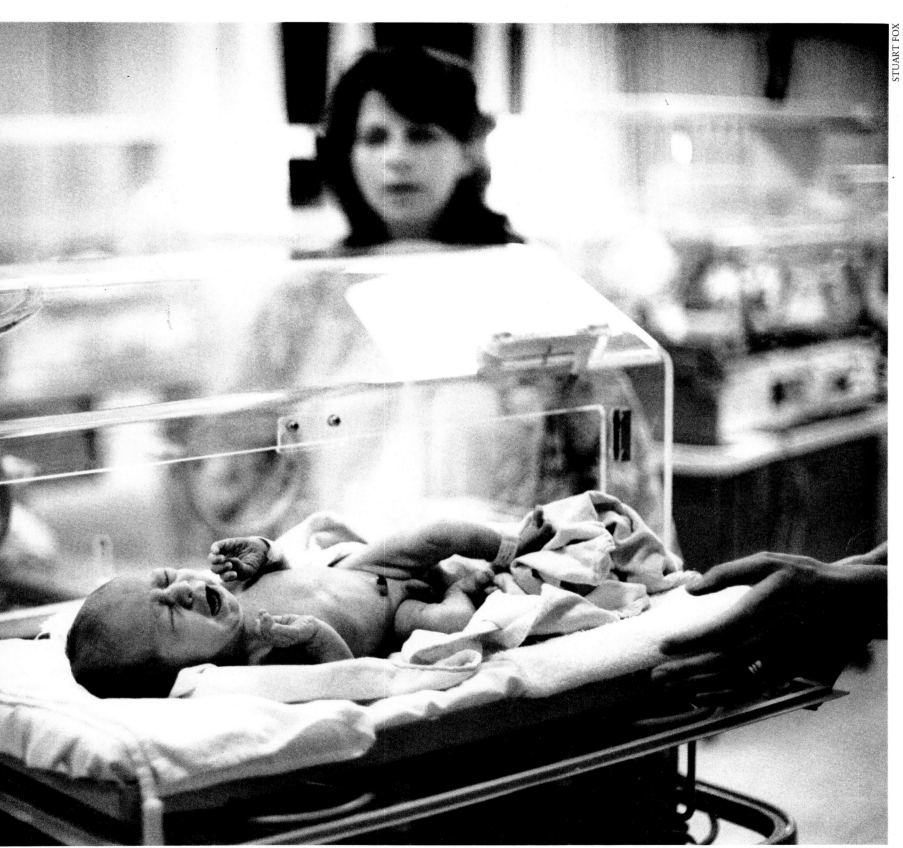

Lismore, New South Wales

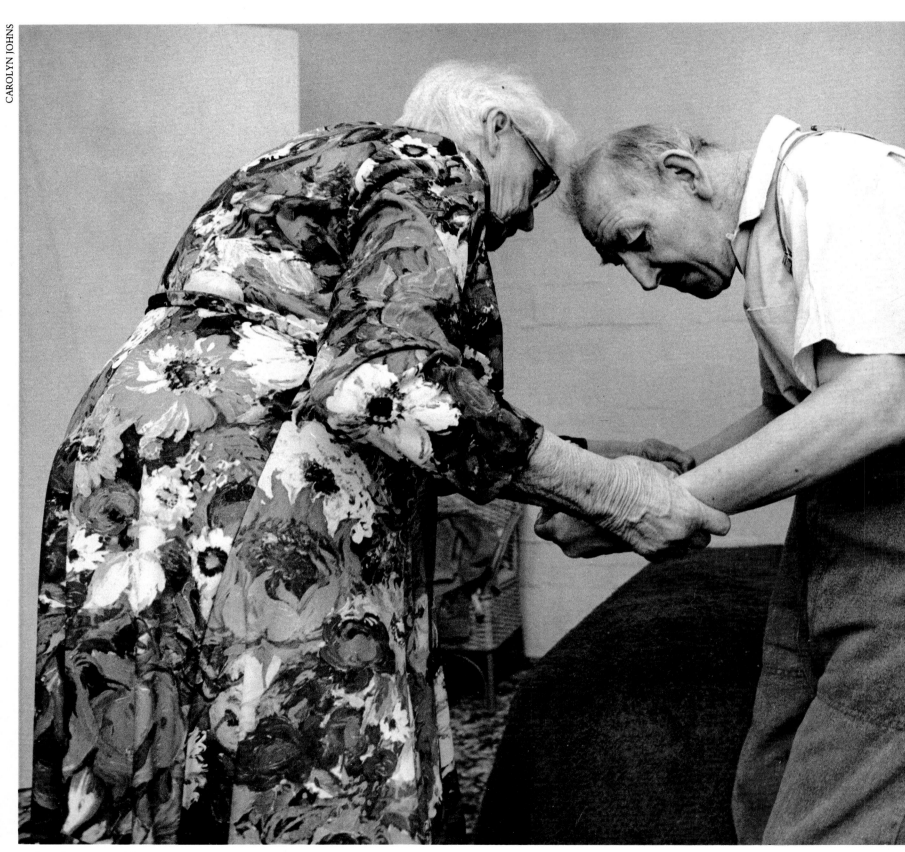

CAROLYN JOHNS

Eighty-three year old Mrs. Christina
Doherty of Numurkah, Victoria, has
taken care of her 62-year-old son, Les,
all his life. He was born physically
handicapped. Approximately 100,000
Australians are handicapped in ways
which require special care.

Above

Mr. Charles Bliss is the 84-year-old
inventor of 'semantography', an international symbol language of 100
characters. Bliss, who has been
refining the language for more than
thirty years, first recognised the need
for a universal symbol language when
he was growing up in Austria.
''People spoke over 20 different
languages in one country,'' he said,
''and there had to be a system where
they could all communicate.''
His 'Blissymbolic' language is
receiving world-wide recognition and
may be a major step in the search for
a global language. It is already used
extensively in the education of the
verbally handicapped.

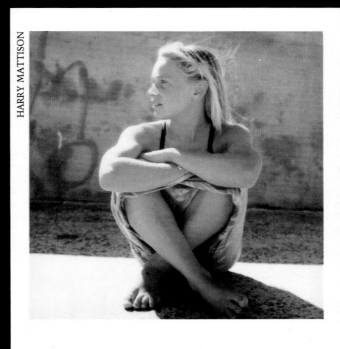

Mining should soon surpass agriculture as Australia's most valuable export industry. But while iron, copper, gold and coal are large, well established industries, the new uranium operations have attracted the attention of a large anti-nuclear movement, concerned with the safe use of radioactive materials in a volatile world.

GREGORY HEISLER

Weano Gorge, Hamersley Range National Park, Western Australia.

Mining magnate Lang Hancock, Western Australia.

Mount Newman, Western Australia

Northern Queensland

In the heart of South Australia's
outback, lies the opal mining town of
Coober Pedy, one of Australia's most
unusual communities. The majority
of the towns' 2000 residents have
elected to live in this 'white fellow's
hole in the ground' in order to shield
themselves from the extremes of
temperature.

5.30 pm

5.30 pm

RUDI MEISEL

Roadtrains link Darwin with rest of Australia in the absence of a railway line. Along the 2000 km stretch of highway between Darwin and Alice Springs these 115 tonne behemoths *(below)* thunder along, with 62 wheels on the ground and up to three trailers tailing behind. The monotony of this endless stretch of road is broken only by small towns and roadside pubs; watering holes where a driver can take a break, have a quick shower, grab a few hours sleep in the back of the cab, and get back on the highway. The Wauchope Hotel, 487 km north of Alice Springs, is a popular stop on the Stuart Highway and driver Wayne Webb *(left)* relaxes there for a moment before continuing north.

Long John Silver's
ICK O'
HE BOX
ZE EVERY TIME
ET RICH QUICK

Long John
Silver's

Claremont Fair, Perth

With most of Australia's population living near the coast, and with all state capitals seaports, it follows that the nation's beaches and waterways attract thousands of visitors. The number of motor boat owners has doubled in the past ten years, and Australia's world-famous yacht race, the Sydney-Hobart, now attracts over 150 entrants, including some of the best ocean-racers in the world.

5.30 pm

BOB DAVIS

STEPHANIE MAZE

The Perth yacht 'Evelyn' was designed to compete in the Sydney-Hobart race. She finished fourth on her first try in 1980.

Left
The Scotch College 'Eight', Yarra River, Melbourne

Far left
Elizabeth Bay, Sydney

GARY CHAPMAN

Charlie Phillott flew back from
Birdsville in time to muster sheep on
Carisbrooke Station. Meanwhile, 1400
km away at Katherine Gorge National
Park, Ranger Peter Torr transports the
day's last load of supplies to an
isolated maintenance team.

'Love is the Drug' is J4 on the juke
box at the Kookaburra Cafe,
Frankston, Victoria.

BRIAN LANKER

Jock and Greg Harold make their own
music on the verandah in Normanton
Queensland.

6.00 pm

LEANNE TEMME

'Time Zone' amusement centre, Perth

Preshil Alternative School students,
Kew, Victoria

ROBIN MOYER

The ANZAC Memorial, Alice Springs

CHEMIST STP
COWRA
PHARMACY

Ford
Cowra
Motors

BANK

Cowra, New South Wales

MIKE O'BRIEN

Three women.
Meekatharra, Western Australia

As the light fades from the sky at New Norcia, Father Justin begins the 140 km drive to Perth in the cool stillness of evening. Across the country the last working day of the week draws to a close and the weekend begins.

Meekatharra, Western Australia

Ruby Francis, 76, of Wittenoom,
Western Australia

The hermit priest, Beagle Bay,
Western Australia.

Sydney

Tullamarine Airport, Melbourne

Canadian photographer Douglas Kirkland, one of the world's leading glamour photographers, has developed a professional interest in astronomy over the past few years. His assignment on March 6 was to photograph the 3.9 m Anglo-Australian telescope at Siding Spring, near Coonabarabran, New South Wales, one of the largest telescopes studying the southern skies and regarded by many astronomers as one of the finest technical instruments in the world. At nearby Parkes, the huge 64 m radio telescope (right) demonstrates another type of astronomy—the study of cosmic radio waves.

'The sky (here) is as black as black can be and there are intense pinpoints of light coming through. It was very exciting. I was shown a Super Nova that had been found the day before. I saw a cluster of more than a million stars. It's hard to tell you the impression the observatory has left with me.'

Control panel operator Roy Howarth,
Mt Tom Price, Western Australia.

8.00 pm

At Melbourne's Moomba Festival *(above)*, the evening's activities are just beginning, while in the Brisbane suburb of West End *(right)*, a bed-time story concludes a busy day.

SARA KRULWICH

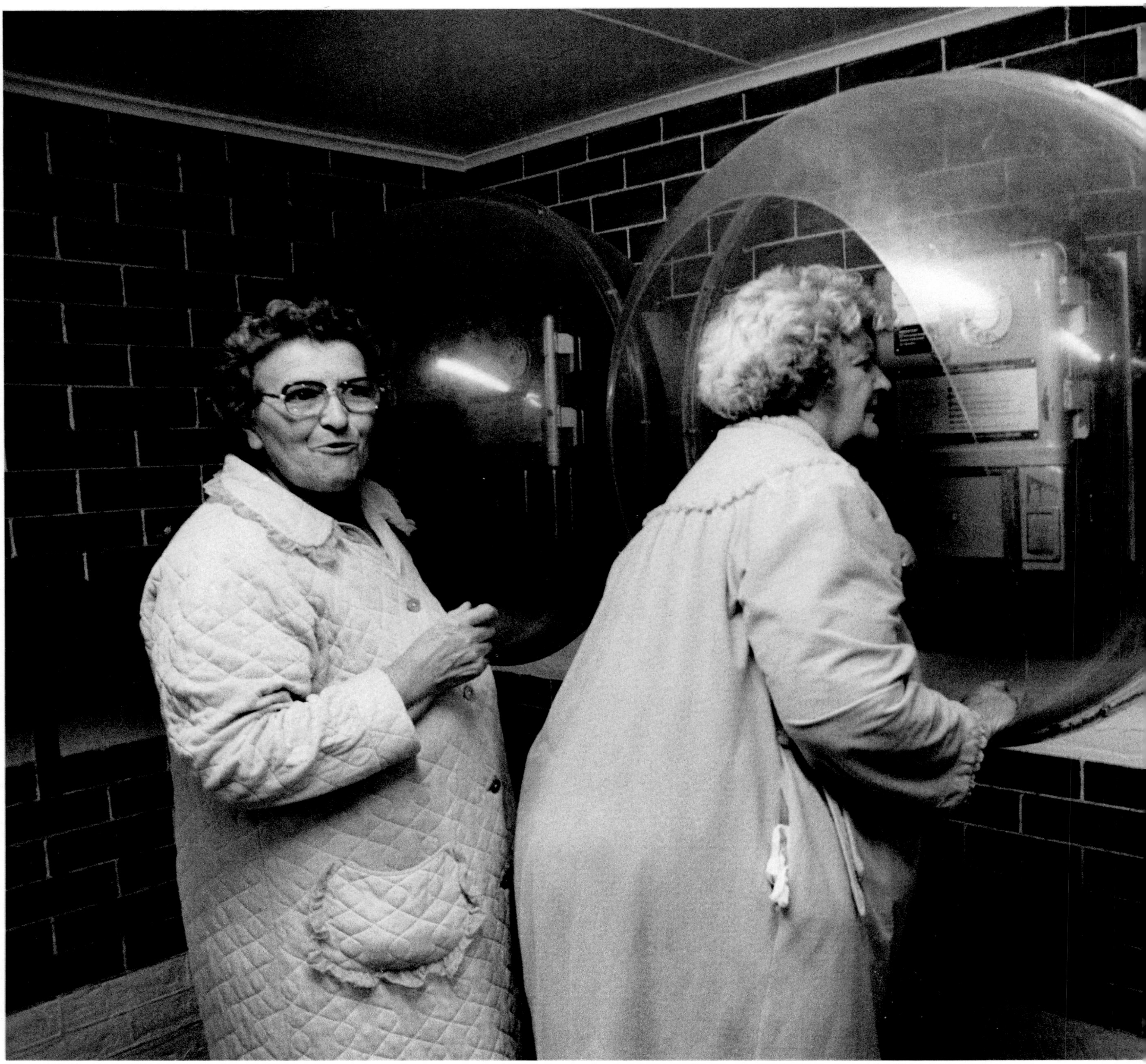

GERD LUDWIG

March 6 has always been a special day for 18-year-old Craig Kibbler of Cowra, New South Wales.

Far left
At Bright, Victoria, campers place one of the 14,729,679 local and STD calls made each day.

Wales

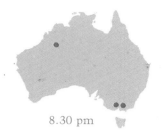

GREGORY HEISLER

To celebrate the end of their first month of teaching, Gary and Margaret Anderson dine *a la carte* at the only restaurant in Mount Tom Price, Western Australia.

Right
With everything home-grown on their Kooroocheang farm in Victoria, vegetarians Helen Wanklyn and Russell Petherbridge treat a 'run-down photojournalist' to organic sunflower seed loaf with fruit sauce, mixed garden salad, and jacket potatoes.

Previous page
At the Barooga Hotel in southern New South Wales, fruit pickers celebrate pay day and the end of the week. In the late 1800s, Australian short story writer and poet Henry Lawson commented on the phenomena of mateship, *'One of the few moments of happiness a man knows in Australia is that moment of meeting the eyes of another man over the tops of two glasses'.*

Myrtle Strong serves up rissoles, boiled potatoes and green beans for husband Russ at the Sunrise Caravan Park, Rosebud, Victoria.

GERD LUDWIG

RSL Club, Cowra, New South Wales

Methodist Ladies College, Melbourne

Royal Exchange Hotel, Toowong,
Queensland

9.30 pm

VLADIMIR SICHOV

Above
Old time dance band, Ballan Victoria

Left
The Lighthouse Squares, Eumundi,
Queensland

LEANNE TEMME

Jo Moore, lead singer with 'The
Fabulairs', Chevron Hotel, Melbourne

Gundaroo Hotel, New South Wales

Cobourg Peninsula, Northern Territory

Random breath testing, Alice Springs,
Northern Territory

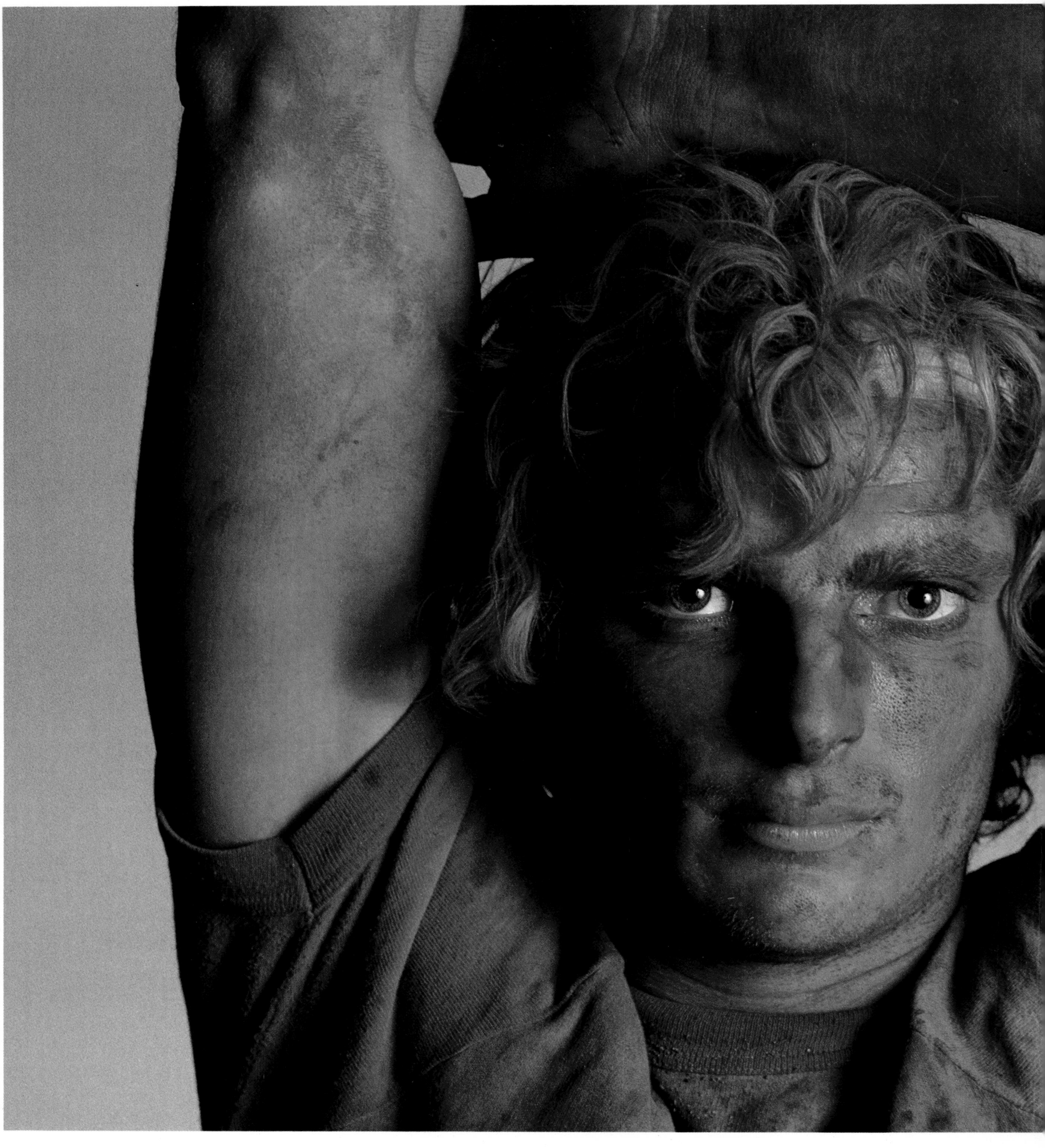

GREGORY HEISLER

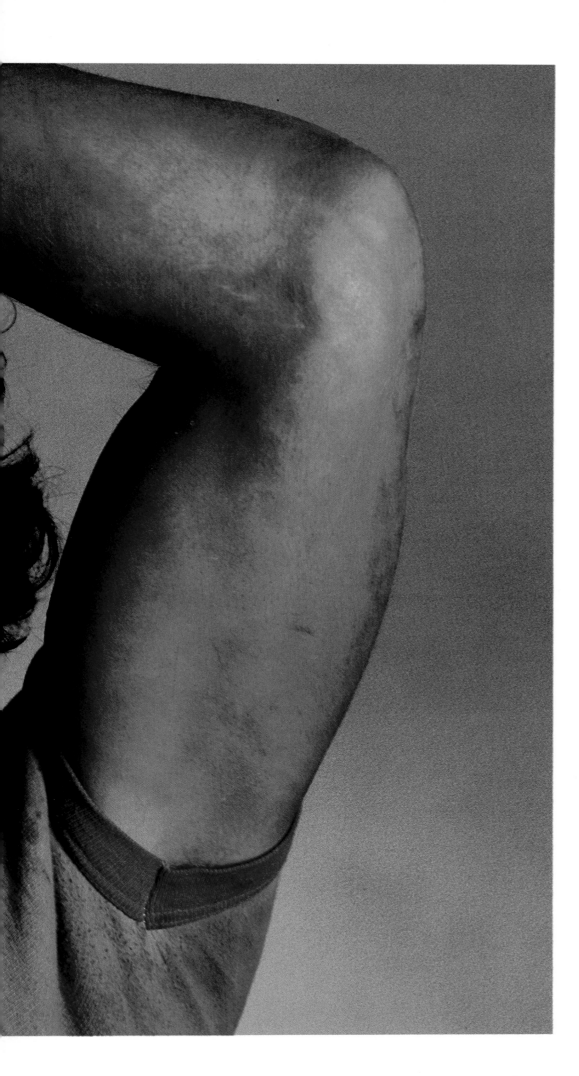

A few minutes before midnight
American photographer Greg Heisler
decided to finish his day of shooting
with a drink in a makeshift canteen
in Yandicoogina. Since dawn he had
shot nearly 40 rolls of film on his
assignment in the Pilbara area of
Western Australia. As he put his
camera gear down he looked around
the small room. In the corner was a
noisy old refrigerator, a pool table,
and a tattered movie screen hanging
from the ceiling.
Roger Gardiner, a young rover with a
drilling team, headed towards the
lights of the canteen. To get a beer
and some conversation he'd just
driven 200 km. 'I've been on the road
since I was 16, working my way
around the country. I've been a store-
man, factory hand, worked on a film
crew, and played keyboards in a rock
band. I like to move alone. It leaves
me free to get into what I want. Right
now I'm putting up with flies, heat,
isolation and hard work to get some
bread together.'
Greg had thought his day of shooting
was over until Roger walked through
the door. The clock read five to
twelve. Heisler dragged down the old
movie screen, set up his lights and
photographed Roger at exactly
midnight.

Following pages
Saturday morning, March 7
At midnight, American photographer
David Burnett set up his tripod and
pointed his camera at Uluru and the
southern sky. He opened the shutter
and waited for five hours, standing
alone in the darkness. As the earth
revolved, the stars registered on the
film as streaks of light around the
immobile monolith. *The Rock
helped me, it is very strong. It has its
own character, its own personality.
It's easier now for me to understand
why there are so many myths and
legends attached to the Rock. Even I
felt haunted by it. I always had the
feeling that I wasn't alone. I always
felt that the Rock was watching back
at me.*

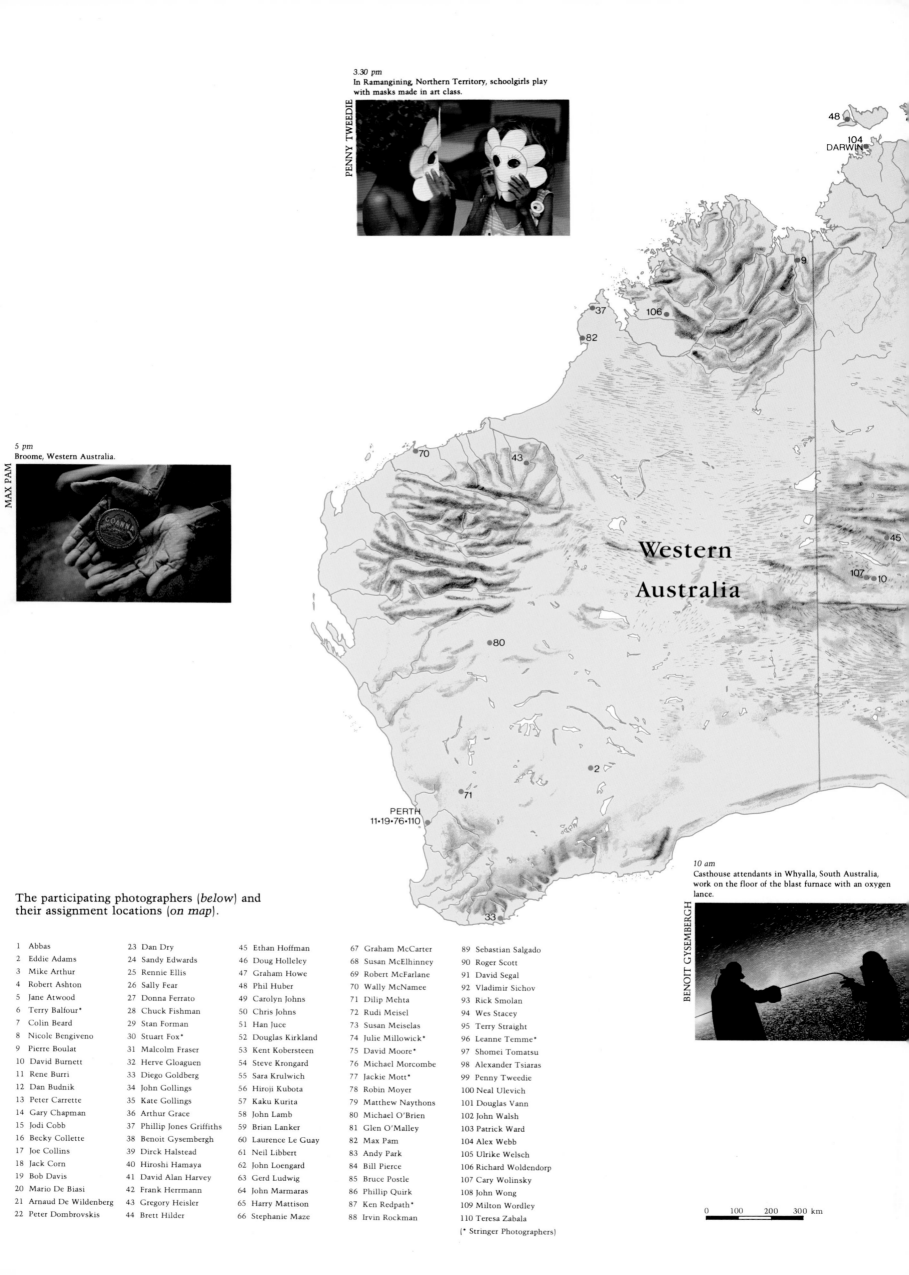

3.30 pm
In Ramangining, Northern Territory, schoolgirls play with masks made in art class.

PENNY TWEEDIE

5 pm
Broome, Western Australia.

MAX PAM

48
104
DARWIN

9

37
106

82

70   43

Western
Australia

45

107 10

80

2

71

PERTH
11·19·76·110

33

10 am
Casthouse attendants in Whyalla, South Australia, work on the floor of the blast furnace with an oxygen lance.

BENOIT GYSEMBERGH

The participating photographers (*below*) and their assignment locations (*on map*).

1 Abbas	23 Dan Dry	45 Ethan Hoffman	67 Graham McCarter	89 Sebastian Salgado
2 Eddie Adams	24 Sandy Edwards	46 Doug Holleley	68 Susan McElhinney	90 Roger Scott
3 Mike Arthur	25 Rennie Ellis	47 Graham Howe	69 Robert McFarlane	91 David Segal
4 Robert Ashton	26 Sally Fear	48 Phil Huber	70 Wally McNamee	92 Vladimir Sichov
5 Jane Atwood	27 Donna Ferrato	49 Carolyn Johns	71 Dilip Mehta	93 Rick Smolan
6 Terry Balfour*	28 Chuck Fishman	50 Chris Johns	72 Rudi Meisel	94 Wes Stacey
7 Colin Beard	29 Stan Forman	51 Han Juce	73 Susan Meiselas	95 Terry Straight
8 Nicole Bengiveno	30 Stuart Fox*	52 Douglas Kirkland	74 Julie Millowick*	96 Leanne Temme*
9 Pierre Boulat	31 Malcolm Fraser	53 Kent Kobersteen	75 David Moore*	97 Shomei Tomatsu
10 David Burnett	32 Herve Gloaguen	54 Steve Krongard	76 Michael Morcombe	98 Alexander Tsiaras
11 Rene Burri	33 Diego Goldberg	55 Sara Krulwich	77 Jackie Mott*	99 Penny Tweedie
12 Dan Budnik	34 John Gollings	56 Hiroji Kubota	78 Robin Moyer	100 Neal Ulevich
13 Peter Carrette	35 Kate Gollings	57 Kaku Kurita	79 Matthew Naythons	101 Douglas Vann
14 Gary Chapman	36 Arthur Grace	58 John Lamb	80 Michael O'Brien	102 John Walsh
15 Jodi Cobb	37 Phillip Jones Griffiths	59 Brian Lanker	81 Glen O'Malley	103 Patrick Ward
16 Becky Collette	38 Benoit Gysembergh	60 Laurence Le Guay	82 Max Pam	104 Alex Webb
17 Joe Collins	39 Dirck Halstead	61 Neil Libbert	83 Andy Park	105 Ulrike Welsch
18 Jack Corn	40 Hiroshi Hamaya	62 John Loengard	84 Bill Pierce	106 Richard Woldendorp
19 Bob Davis	41 David Alan Harvey	63 Gerd Ludwig	85 Bruce Postle	107 Cary Wolinsky
20 Mario De Biasi	42 Frank Herrmann	64 John Marmaras	86 Phillip Quirk	108 John Wong
21 Arnaud De Wildenberg	43 Gregory Heisler	65 Harry Mattison	87 Ken Redpath*	109 Milton Wordley
22 Peter Dombrovskis	44 Brett Hilder	66 Stephanie Maze	88 Irvin Rockman	110 Teresa Zabala
				(* Stringer Photographers)

0   100   200   300 km

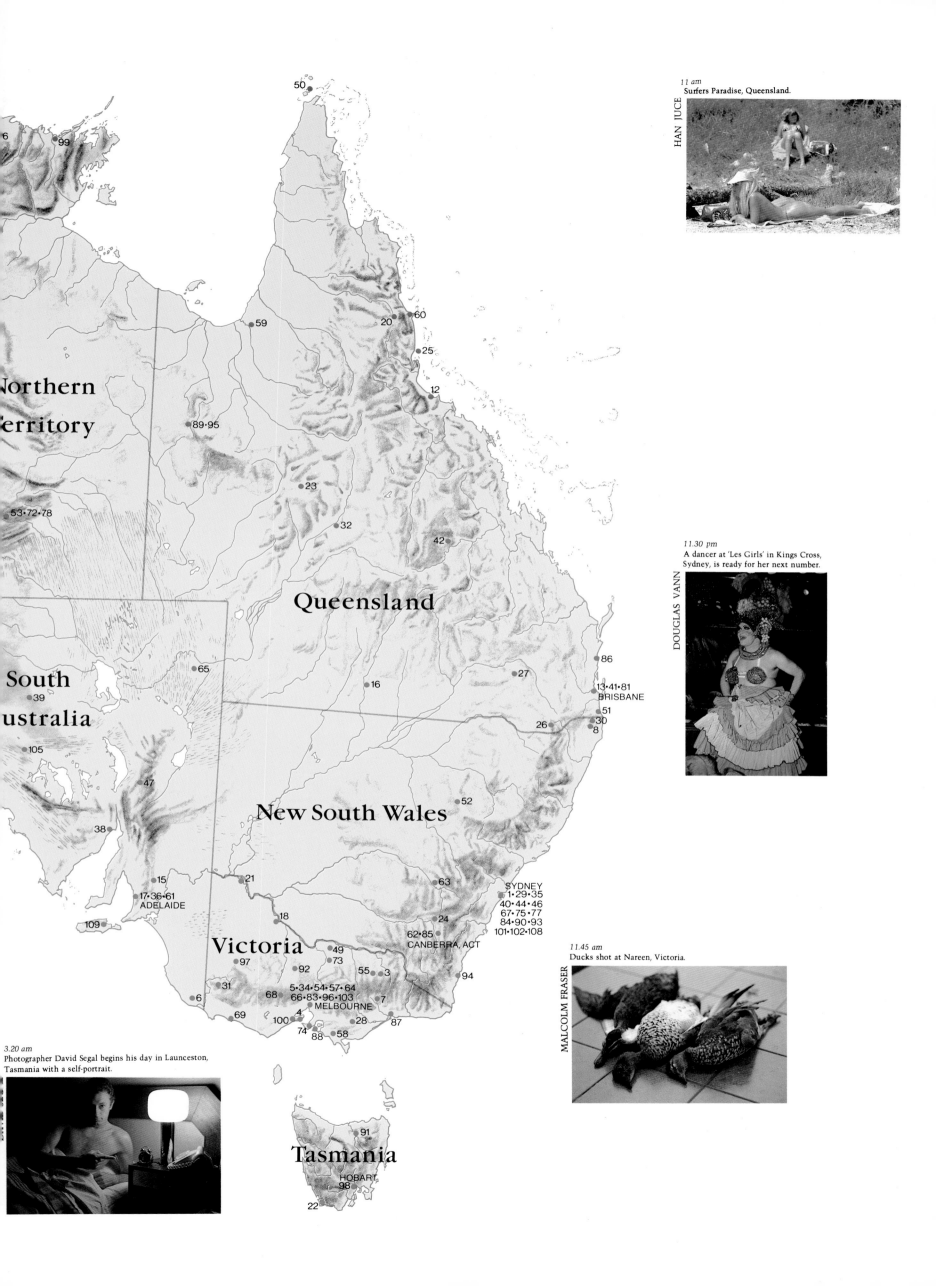

11 am
Surfers Paradise, Queensland.

HAN JUCE

11.30 pm
A dancer at 'Les Girls' in Kings Cross,
Sydney, is ready for her next number.

DOUGLAS VANN

11.45 am
Ducks shot at Nareen, Victoria.

MALCOLM FRASER

3.20 am
Photographer David Segal begins his day in Launceston,
Tasmania with a self-portrait.

6 ● 99

Northern
Territory

53•72•78

● 50

● 59   ● 20 ●60

● 25

12

● 89•95

● 23

● 32

42

Queensland

● 65

● 16   ● 27   ● 86

13•41•81
BRISBANE

● 51
● 30
8

● 26

South
Australia

● 39

● 105

● 47

● 52

● 38

New South Wales

● 15
17•36•61
ADELAIDE   ● 21   ● 63

SYDNEY
● 1•29•35
40•44•46
67•75•77
84•90•93
101•102•108

● 109   ● 18   ● 24

62•85
CANBERRA, ACT

● 49   ● 94
Victoria   ● 73

● 97   ● 92   ● 55   ● 3

● 31   5•34•54•57•64   ● 7
● 6   68   66•83•96•103
● 69   4   MELBOURNE   ● 28   ● 87
● 100
74   88   58

● 91

Tasmania

HOBART
98

● 22

A Day in the Life of Australia photographers pose for Gregory Heisler (*in mirror*) shortly before leaving Sydney on their assignments.

DITLA Revisited

MARCH 1, 1981. Another perfect evening in Sydney. It had been 32°C during the day and as the sun went down a gentle breeze blew into the city. Outside the Tai Yuen Palace on Sussex Street, 48 people pile out of a hired bus and crowd into the restaurant, laughing and joking like old friends reunited for a special occasion. Inside, the air of festivity grows as countless bottles of Riesling are passed around a makeshift banquet table. A rock and roll band plays as plates full of oriental delicacies come and go, punctuated by dancing, laughter and chatter in English, French, Spanish, German and Italian.

At the far end of the table a long-haired young man peers at the group, adjusting his wire-framed glasses, attempting to take it all in. Rick Smolan is having trouble believing that the scene before him is real. He is surrounded by men and women who, like himself, are photographers. Some of them are old friends, others telephone acquaintances. Some of them he knows only by reputation. For an instant, Smolan thinks he must be dreaming. Then he realises that it couldn't be a dream—he hasn't been near a bed in 72 hours.

This Chinese banquet was one of many spontaneous celebrations which occurred when photographers from all over the world met, for the first time in history, to take part in an unlikely sounding project called 'A Day in the Life of Australia'. Their presence was the fulfilment of a dream that Smolan and his partner, Andy Park, had been nurturing for two years. With a combination of perseverance, industry, luck, and the help of some very good friends, they had somehow made it come true. They had been so busy writing letters, making phone calls, arguing, pleading and overdrawing their bank accounts, that they had no time to speculate on what it would really be like to have 100 world-famous photographers all in the same place, at the same time.

The 67 photographers who came from abroad to join 33 Australians in documenting a 24-hour period in the life of this vast country, range in age from 25 to 65, and have in common a love of their profession, strong enough to make what Australian advertising photographer John Gollings calls the 'leap of faith' necessary to accept this unbelievable sounding assignment. Their backgrounds are varied; they are Pulitzer prize winners, staffers and contributors to the world's major magazines, prize winning newspaper photographers, a few come from the fashion and advertising fields.

They came despite the fact that it meant passing up lucrative jobs, or committing themselves to a week in a distant country where a flash-flood is a major news event. What would have happened if real news had broken while all the people who usually cover it were tied up, all on the same assignment? But 100 of the world's leading photographers decided to accept the challenge and spend a week down under.

In the months before the photographers arrived, Andy Park's house in Melbourne became general headquarters for what was then an abstract beast called 'A Day in the Life of Australia'— soon to be known by its initials— DITLA—because the full title was too long to say more than once on a long-distance phone call. Park's

Project Directors Rick Smolan (left) and Andy Park (right)

living room became the command post, where a huge map was adorned with 100 coloured tacks indicating photographers' names and assignments. The telex machine began to kick on frequently—often in the middle of the night—and Park and his friends learned to sleep through the rat-tat-tat of messages being transmitted across thousands of kilometres and dozens of time zones. Near the telex machine someone had hung a xeroxed message cynically defining the six stages of a project: 1) wild enthusiasm, 2) total confusion, 3) disillusionment, 4) search for the guilty, 5) punishment of the innocent, 6) promotion of non-participants.

Smolan and Park had no idea of the immensity of the task they had taken on. 'We figured it would take at least three or four months to organise the whole thing,' Smolan remembers, 'and that was two years ago.' Once a date was set for the arrival of the photographers, there were periods when it seemed as if they would

never make it. 'It was like barrelling down a steep hillside on the back of a flat-bed truck,' Smolan explains, 'you're headed for the edge of a huge cliff and desperately trying to build an airplane on the back of the truck before you go over.' But everytime disaster seemed certain, something miraculous happened to rescue the floundering project. Financing was the foremost problem. BP Australia offered to underwrite the project and got it off the ground and running. Then, one by one, corporate sponsors agreed to back DITLA. At the last minute Smolan and Park developed a staff—a devoted crew of volunteers who applied their various skills to tackling the countless administrative tasks that had been put off due to lack of time, money and

manpower. Lyne Helms, a film producer who became the project's co-ordinator, pointed out that the logistics of setting up such an ambitious project were exactly the same as producing a movie. What was needed were the skills of film production managers. The only difference between co-ordinating the project and producing a feature film was that in this case the final product was a book instead of a movie. The amount of work involved was identical.

Late in February Qantas ground-crews went out on strike putting most of their fleet of 747s temporarily out of commission. It looked like DITLA was really doomed. 'I actually felt a wave of relief when the strike came up,' says Smolan. 'I thought: maybe we'll have a few week's extra time now, or maybe they won't come at all and we can just call the whole thing off.' But the photographers were already wiring and phoning to say they'd be there. In one of many eleventh-hour saves, Qantas arranged alternative flights. A representative was sent to

California to make sure that the 'zoo flight', a jet carrying 49 US-based photographers, left San Francisco on schedule.

The logistics of DITLA defied all the natural and man-made rules of business where Murphy's Law usually prevails. Kodak came through at the last minute with film stock, and the Hyatt Kingsgate donated all the hotel rooms, and a large conference room. After weeks of trying to raise enough money to produce a documentary film about the project, the DITLA staff had finally given up. The day before the photographers arrived a film finance group heard about DITLA and agreed to underwrite the entire documentary. By the time the photographers arrived, accommodations had been arranged, their individual kits had been prepared with film, identification numbers, maps, and schedules. Co-ordinators in each of Australia's States and Territories had worked with Rick and Andy and managed to develop and research an assignment for each photographer. Enough TAA flights had been secured to send 100 photographers criss-crossing the continent.

Most of the DITLA photographers were accustomed to heavy travel schedules and last minute arrangements. Many are like 28-year-old Dilip Mehta, an Indian photographer who lives in Canada but spends more time on 747s than in his apartment. But while many of them had worked extensively on every other continent, the majority had never been to Australia. More surprising was the fact that while the world's leading photojournalists had been reading each other's names and admiring one another's work for years, many of them had never met. They had crossed paths in hotel lobbies or shaken hands in the offices of magazines and picture agencies, but few had ever spent any time together. Theirs is a nomadic existence. Like American Jodi Cobb of *National Geographic* who says, 'while other women are waiting by the phone for a date, I'm waiting in a hotel room for my four o'clock wake-up call.'

The first four days in Sydney had been set aside to give the photographers time to relax and get to know one another. And as each day passed there was a growing camaraderie that came with the knowledge that this was a collaboration, not a competition. English photographer Phillip Jones-Griffiths' opening remarks at the Philip Morris Photographic Seminar reinforced this sense of community.

'Before we start this seminar, the first thing I'd like to do is

Greg Heisler photographs the other 99 photographers on the steps of the Sydney Opera House (page 278-279)

Picture editors (Terry Le Goubin, Dorean Davis, Designer Adrian Young, Michael Rand, Steve Ettlinger) looking at a selection of the 96,000 photographs shot on March 6.

read to you a letter published in the current issue of *Newsweek* magazine written by an Indian gentleman from Bombay. *In a local newspaper I saw a picture of the late photographer Olivier Rebbot lying injured in El Salvador whilst on assignment for Newsweek. I was moved by Rebbot's commitment to his job. I began questioning my commitment to my own job. I own a movie theatre. What had I contributed to people's lives? I was not happy with the answer. That picture of Rebbot now is placed on my office wall. Everytime I want to retreat from a certain stance in which courage is required, that photograph will give me strength to face what I must.*
Well, Olivier was supposed to be here today, he was one of the 100 photographers asked to come to Australia to partake in the project. Many of us here have worked with him, and some very closely indeed—in fact the person who was with him when the sniper's bullet hit him in the chest, whilst they were together on a street in El Salvador—that person is actually sitting here this morning, and for him and others who knew Olivier well in El Salvador, the loss is particularly hard to bear.'
The seminar marked a change in the mood of the group. As the work of their peers was projected, the party atmosphere of the first few days began to fade. 'We are all awed at being at the same place at the same time' said Sarah Krulwich of the New York *Times*, 'and we are all very nervous.' Everyone seemed to feel anxiety about the formidable quality of the competition. Imagine the pressure: in only 24 hours, 100 dedicated professionals had to live up to the

reputations that had earned them invitations to DITLA. On the third day in Sydney, a gangly young man sporting a pink shirt and a dapper straw hat appeared in the lobby of the Hyatt. Still yawning after an 11-hour flight from Tokyo, Greg Heisler, an American whose hallmark is his willingness to work constantly, arrived late because he had been covering the Pope's visit to Japan. He was just in time to take the only group portrait of all the photographers as they gathered at dusk on the steps of the Sydney Opera House.
The next day Smolan addressed the group before their departure to assigned locations. He encouraged everyone to stay up for the 24 hours on March 6, to shoot as much as humanly possible and added that film shot during the four-day research period might be considered, but must be labelled with the date it was shot. He pleaded with everyone to label and caption their work as accurately and in as much detail as possible.

Eddie Adams

The task of sorting it all out afterwards was going to be difficult enough without chasing photographers around the world for caption information. 'You will be very hard to reach once you leave Australia. Some of you were almost impossible to track down in the first place.' When Smolan concluded, he was given a standing ovation. 'I don't know how Smolan and Park did it' said *National Geographic's* David Alan Harvey, surveying the room full of cheering photographers, 'I can't even get my friends at the *Geographic* together for lunch.'
'I know of nothing comparable in the history of photography,' Canadian Douglas Kirkland remarked later. 'There has been no bitching or whining and there is a feeling of brotherhood that I've never experienced before.' In a business that thrives on competition, whose stars are loners and individualists, a group effort of this scope had never before been attempted. The photographers

Susan Meiselas

demonstrated their professionalism by not only using their talents, but sharing them. John Lamb, who has worked at a Melbourne paper for 27 years was one photographer who was not entirely pleased with the assignment he was given. He thought there was little hope of 'getting anything new' out of an assignment 'right in my own back-yard.' The strength of the images he turned in attests to an assumption that was one of the premises of DITLA from the start: A good photojournalist's eye does not become jaded. In effect, this was the challenge facing each of the DITLA photographers: to take a subject (i.e. Ayers Rock), which people have photographed from every conceivable angle and show that subject in a new light. To push past all the cliches and super-ficialities and create one-of-a-kind images in only 24 hours.
The photojournalists selected for DITLA are accustomed to working under pressure. They are used to documenting all aspects of life, photographing far more than just wars and disasters. They not only create a visual record for history, they communicate subtle infor-mation about what life is like on one side of the world to people living on the other. On March 6, 100 such photographers woke up on farms and fishing boats, in motels and monasteries all over the country. They took off in the chartered planes and helicopters, rented cars and borrowed Land-rovers which were waiting for them when they set out to look at Australia.
When the photographers completed their assignments they turned in their film and told of their adventures in individual taped debriefing sessions. Some returned to Sydney while others left immediately for their next assignments.

Ten days after meeting each other, photographer Greg Heisler and his new wife Prudence Taubert pose for a wedding photograph on the steps of the Sydney Opera House.

*Brazilian Sebastian Salgado flew directly to the US to do a story on President Reagan for the New York *Times*. Salgado and fellow photographer Dirck Halstead were on the scene at the Hilton Hotel and moved quickly enough to capture the assassination attempt on film.

*Australian Carolyn Johns began shooting photographs for a National Times article titled 'Sex in Australia'.

*American Matthew Naythons arrived in Thailand the day the revolution broke out and covered it for the New York Times.

*Australian Kate and John Gollings headed off for Sri Lanka to shoot an advertising campaign for Air Lanka.

*American Arthur Grace left for Poland to cover the workers revolt for *Time* magazine.

*Australian Bob Davis flew to South Australia to shoot a story on the wine industry for the London Sunday *Times*.

*American Susan Meiselas returned to New York for the launching of her book document-

ing two years in Nicaragua.

*American Harry Mattison returned to El Salvador to shoot a cover story on the revolution for *Time* magazine.

*Iranian photographer Abbas returned to Paris to find he had received the first Olivier Rebbot award for photojournalism.

*Japanese photographer Hiroji Kubota returned home to receive his country's Photographer of the Year award.

*Australian John Marmaras spent two weeks with his family in Melbourne and then returned to New York to shoot the Annual Directors' Meeting for Citibank.

*American Doug Vann travelled to Atlanta, Georgia, to shoot a story for the *Village Voice* on Atlanta's reaction to the brutal murders of 21 black children.

Meanwhile, back in Sydney, film was beginning to roll in from the labs, and the editors were faced with an awesome task. Michael Rand of the London Sunday *Times*, Dorean Davis of *Newsweek*, Steve Ettlinger of *Geo*, and Terence LeGoubin of the

Colorific Picture Agency had flown in just in time to miss The Day and be faced with the results: 2,384 rolls of film that had to be pared down to 350 images in less than two weeks. Like everything else about 'A Day in the Life' the grand scale became part of the overall aesthetic. Each of the 96,000 photographs had to be stamped with each individual photographer's identification number. 'The process is mind boggling,' Ettlinger confessed. 'There are so many images here you could make three or four great books out of what we've got.' Forty photographers volunteered to stay on and help stamp and edit. That left a core group in Sydney, not unlike the one that had occupied the Hyatt during the first four days of DITLA. They edited all day, every day.

Every night there was a 'farewell party' for a photographer who planned to move on the next day. Then Greg Heisler appeared again. He had stayed on in Perth nursing the eye infection he'd developed on assignment. That night at

dinner he met Pru Taubert, an Australian psychotherapist. Five days later he took Smolan aside and asked if he could possibly find the time to take some pictures at a wedding. 'Whose wedding?' Smolan asked. 'Mine' Heisler replied. Heisler and Taubert were married 10 days after they met. They posed for wedding portraits on the steps of the Opera House where three weeks earlier Heisler had taken a picture of the 100 photographers. The romance between Heisler and Taubert was one of many indications that DITLA was more than just a convention for world-weary photographers or two ambitious photographers' scheme to promote Australia. Long before this book went to press—even before the film started coming back from the laboratory—everyone associated with DITLA knew that they had taken part in something strange and wonderful.

In that last briefing Smolan had said 'we have tried to make this as challenging for you as possible,' and the project certainly succeeded in that respect. He also said 'I hope this will set some precedent,' which it undoubtedly will, now that he and Park have proven that all it takes is determination to do the impossible.

The project took a degree of daring which even Smolan admits consisted more of naïveté than nerve. 'If we had known how much work this was going to be,' he said several times, 'we would never have started it.'

Amy M. Schiffman
Assistant Editor
American Photographer Magazine

Only a week after leaving Australia, Brazilian Photographer Sebastian Salgado and American Photographer Dirck Halstead were both on the scene when President Reagan was shot in Washington D.C. Their photographs appeared in Time Magazine (left) and Newsweek (right).

DITLA Biographies

Iran 1978
Abbas   **France**
'The last picture I took was the most significant. Outside of a house in Redfern was a group of aborigines drinking, a very sad scene. These people had lost their culture, they are not white and I don't think they were blacks either. Australia? I didn't get any real feeling, negative or positive. It didn't arouse any great passion in me.'
A 'third worlder' transplanted to the West, Abbas has covered Africa, the Middle East and Asia for the past 10 years. His major stories include Biafra, Vietnam, Ethiopia, the Arab/Israeli conflict and the Iranian revolution. Shortly after DITLA he won the first Olivier Rebbot Award. He is associated with the Magnum Photo Agency.

Saigon 1969
Eddie Adams   **USA**
'I headed straight for Hay Street in Kalgoorlie. I wanted my 9 am business shot to be the Madam and her girls. First I talked to Stella who sent me to Mona. Mona passed me on to Irene who agreed to pose for the picture. When I showed up at 9 am on the sixth, Irene had been arrested.'
Adams has received more than 400 awards for his photographic work in the United States and overseas, including the 1969 Pulitzer Prize for News Photography. In 1975, he won the American National Press Photographer's Association award for Magazine Photographer of the Year. He is one of the founding members of Contact Press Images.

Michael Arthur   **Australia**
Arthur is currently the Melbourne picture editor for *The Australian*. His work on the Essendon air crash won his pictures worldwide distribution.

Robert Ashton   **Australia**
Ashton is a graduate in photography from the Prahran College of Technology. His work was selected for the United Nations 'habitat' conference in 1976.

Jane Evelyn Atwood   **USA**
'Everything in Australia seemed to be borrowed from somewhere else. It had no soul. It was very new, like America at the beginning. It was beautiful, friendly, open. I felt free. But I wouldn't want to live there.'
From 1976 to 1978 Atwood specialised in photographing 'marginal' people. In 1980 she won the first Eugene Smith Memorial Grant for Humanistic Photo-

graphy. An exhibition of her work on blind children was featured at the International Center for Photography in New York City in October 1981.

New South Wales 1980
Colin Beard   **Australia**
After many years of commercial work, Beard now specialises in photojournalism and education. His reportage appears frequently in magazines, and he holds regular classes at the Sydney College of the Arts. In 1973, he won the Gold Medal of the New York Art Directors' Club. His first book, *The Mountain Men*, was published in 1982.

Nicole Bengiveno   **USA**
A staff photographer for the *San Francisco Examiner* since 1977, Bengiveno was named 1979 News Photographer of the Year by the San Francisco Press Photographer's Association.

Pierre Boulat   **France**
'Australia is almost a paradise. The real surprise is the treatment of aboriginals. There is a real problem. Why a big fight with nature? They introduce a bug to eat the insect and then they need a bird to eat the bug.'
Boulat has been travelling extensively throughout Europe, the Middle East and Africa, working as a freelancer and under contract for major international magazines including 23 years with *Life*.

Dan Budnik   **USA**
Budnik has taken photos for most of the world's leading international magazines, including *National Geographic*, *Look*, *Life*, *Newsweek*, *Time*, *Fortune*, *Geo*, *Town* and *Country*, *L'Express*, *Paris-Match* and *Stern*.

Iran 1979
David Burnett   **USA**
Burnett received the Overseas Press Club's Robert Capa Gold Medal for his coverage of the aftermath of the Chilean *coup d'etat* in 1973. In 1980 he won a number of major prizes: Press Photo of the Year in the World Press Photo Competition in Amsterdam; Magazine Photographer of the Year by the NPPA; and Best Photographic Reporting from Abroad from the Overseas Press Club of New York. He is one of the founding members of Contact Press Images.

Rene Burri   **Switzerland**
Burri has worked for most of the world's leading magazines including *Life*, *Stern* and The Sunday *Times*, and is also an accomplished film maker. He

received the 1967 New York International Film & Television Award for a film on the Xerox Corporation. He is a member of the Magnum Photo Agency.

Peter Carrette   **UK**
Since the mid-1970s Carrette has specialised in fashion and beauty photography. His various assignments for magazines such as *Australian Playboy*, *Cleo*, *Pol* and *Vogue Australia* together with advertising work for cosmetic and fashion agencies, has taken him to the USA, France, Italy and Europe.

Gary Chapman   **USA**
Chapman, a staff photographer for the Fort Myers *News-Press* in Florida, has won awards in Pictures of the Year competitions from the Florida Press Club and the National Press Photographers Association.

Jodi Cobb   **USA**
'The Barossa Valley was the first time I've ever seen an entire valley run as a public relations movement. Big business rather than little vineyards. I was surprised to see the small growers selling their grapes to the wine producers and not making wine for themselves.'
A staff photographer for the National Geographic Society since 1978, Cobb has won numerous awards for her work and was runner-up in the Magazine Photographer of the Year competition in 1979.

Rebecca Collette   **USA**
'My first impression of Cunnummula was pulling up in small aircraft, jumping out, and getting besieged by thousands of flies all over my body. The people live really out on the edge. No cities, no towns. They do things, like slitting a sheep's throat, as a matter of course—it's their livelihood, their food. You have to be hard to survive. They were very gracious and generous people. It's triumphant that they can live there, make it work and really enjoy it.'
Collette won the Robert F. Kennedy Photographic Awards in 1978 and 1979, and has contributed to two books, *Women See Men* and *Our Day and Generation* by Senator Edward Kennedy. Her work on Women in the Military appeared in GEO Magazine.

Joseph Collins   **Australia**
In 1965 Collins placed both first and fourth in the Asahi Pentax International Photographic competition which attracted one-and-a-half million entries. He has since won numerous awards from photographic societies and royal shows.

Jack Corn   **USA**
One of the senior figures in American news photography, his work has appeared in *Time*, the New York *Times*, *Life*, the Philadelphia *Enquirer*, *Newsweek*, Associated Press and United Press International. The recipient of numerous awards in photojournalism, he is presently Professor of Photojournalism at Western Kentucky University.

Bob Davis   **Australia**
Davis has exhibited in Japan and Australia and recently published a book called *Faces of Japan*. In 1981 he started

a photographic agency called 'The Stock House' in Hong Kong.

Mario De Biasi   **Italy**
De Biasi has worked as chief photographer of Italy's leading picture magazine, Epoca, since 1953. His photographs have appeared on hundreds of magazine covers and his assignments have ranged from natural disasters to portraits of famous personalities.

Arnaud De Wildenberg   **France**
De Wildenberg is best known for his coverage of the Afghanistan crisis, Iranian and Cambodian refugees and the famine in Uganda. He won the *Paris-Match* contest for the best news report in 1980 for his work in Uganda.

Peter Dombrovskis   **Australia**
Dombrovski's close friendship with the late Olegas Truchanas—noted Tasmanian explorer, photographer and conservationist was the inspiration for his present commitment to wilderness photography.

Dan Dry   **USA**
'I got a lift out of Winton with two old bushmen. We must have gone a 100 miles over this dirt track without exchanging one word. I was just dozing off when we passed a car—the second thing we had passed all day. And suddenly the guy driving broke the silence. "Never seen so much traffic on this road before" he said.'
Dry is the only photographer to be twice named Photographer of the Year in the Atlanta Southern Seminar on Photojournalism. His photographs have appeared in *Time*, *Newsweek*, *National Geographic* and several other major magazines and publications.

Sandy Edwards   **New Zealand**
'I usually photograph women but the landowners at the races were much more picturesque than the ladies. The men were quite charming in their hats, tweed coats and moleskin pants'.
Edwards' many exhibitions include Women and Society—Sydney University, Arnhemland Children—Polaroid Exhibition, City of Sydney Festival, and Women & Sport Exhibition.

Victoria 1975
Rennie Ellis   **Australia**
A freelance photojournalist of wide experience, Ellis' books include *Australian Graffiti* and *King's Cross*. His reportage frequently appears overseas or in Australian magazines such as the *Bulletin*, *Pol*, *Playboy*, *Vogue*, *National Review* and *Penthouse*.

Sally Fear   **UK**
In 1975 Fear won the first Royal Photographic Society Nikon Scholarship and her pictures have since appeared in the Sunday *Times* Magazine, the *Observer Colour* Magazine, and the Sunday *Telegraph* Magazine.

San Francisco 1979

Donna Ferrato   **USA**

'They make a remarkable breed of men in Queensland. They just love their women to pieces. I want to get myself one.'

Ferrato is a visitor from another galaxy sent here to observe life on earth. Under the guise of photojournalism she has explored the French passion for bread, America's move into the erotic arena, and the mating habits of celebrities. Her work appears frequently in *Esquire* and *Attenzione*.

Chuck Fishman   **USA**

Fishman has produced cover stories for *Life, Time, Fortune,* and the London Sunday *Times,* as well as book covers for the Pope's visits to France and the USA. Exhibitions of his work have been held in the major American galleries as well as in Europe. He is associated with Contact Press Images.

Boston 1975

Stan Forman   **USA**

Forman is the only photographer in history to receive the Pulizer Prize for News Photography two years in a row (1975 and 1976). He works for the Boston *Herald American* and is described as a news photographer who has an exceptional instinct for top news stories. He has just completed a year at Harvard on a Nieman Scholarship.

Nareen March 6, 1981

Malcolm Fraser   **Australia**

Malcolm Fraser has been Prime Minister of Australia since 1975. Despite his busy schedule, he has not only maintained a keen personal interest in photography, but has also helped foster the development of the Australian photographic industry as a whole.

Herve Gloaguen   **France**

'I like the way Australian people are relaxed, the way they dress and just be themselves. They aren't out to impress. When I was in Longreach I saw a pet emu next door to the motel— it had run away. The owner, a lady, was trying to get 'snookums' to come home. Not an easy thing to do. It was a very funny place'.

Gloaguen has held one-man exhibitions of his work at the Musee d'Art Moderne in Paris, the Glaerie Gloux and several other of France's leading galleries. Collections of his work appear in The Bibliotheque Nationale de Paris, and The Musee Niecephore.

Francios Mitterand 1978

Diego Goldberg   **Argentina**

After starting photojournalism in Latin America as a correspondent for Camera Press, Goldberg moved to the Paris office in 1977, and then to New York in 1980. Now with the Sygma Photo Agency, his work has been featured in major magazines throughout the world.

John Gollings   **Australia**

Gollings is a freelance photographer best known for his architectural documentation, advertising work and candid location photography.

Kate Gollings   **Australia**

Gollings' work has been exhibited extensively throughout Australia and she also operates a custom photographic printing laboratory in Melbourne (her laboratory printed the black and white prints for *A Day in the Life of Australia).*

Arthur Grace   **USA**

'Adelaide? I loved it. I'm on the first plane out. Found the worst restaurant in the world where the house special was second shelf down, third bottle to the left.'

Grace has covered stories ranging from Northern Ireland and drought in western Africa to the 1973 Middle East war. His photos have appeared in *Time, Life, Look, Newsweek,* London Sunday *Times, Paris-Match, Epoca* and *Bunte.* He is associated with the Sygma Photo Agency.

Benoit Gysembergh   **France**

Gysembergh began his career covering the revolution in Portugal for Gamma. He went on to Lebanon to cover the civil war, then photographed the revolutions in El Salvador and Nicaragua, as well as documenting the plight of child labourers in Columbian coal mines.

Dirck Halstead   **USA**

'Safety regulations in Coober Pedy are what they decide upon that day. Mario made his charges by rolling the explosives in newspaper and then lighting the fuse with the end of his cigarette. It's a hard way to gamble.'

Halstead has spent more than 20 years covering major news events throughout the world, first for UPI and then for *Time* Magazine. His major awards include the Robert Capa Award, first place in 1974 New York Press Association, and the White House News Photographers' Association Award in 1976 and 1977.

Hiroshi Hamaya   **Japan**

Hamaya was born in 1915 and started his professional photographic career at the age of 16. A retrospective exhibition of 50 years of his unique work toured the major cities of the world in 1981. Eight weeks after DITLA he won the 1981 Shincho Sha Gran Prix Award for Fine Arts.

David Alan Harvey   **USA**

Harvey obtained his Bachelor's Degree in art journalism from Virginia Commonwealth Univeristy, and then did graduate work at the University of Missouri. He is presently a staff photographer for *National Geographic.*

Gregory Heisler   **USA**

Heisler has freelanced for many major international and American magazines including *Life, GEO, Fortune* and the New York *Times.*

Frank Herrmann   **UK**

Herrmann has been a staff photographer for the London Sunday *Times* since 1963 and has travelled extensively for both the newspaper and the magazine sections.

Brett Hilder   **Australia**

For 20 years Hilder has worked in film, theatre, and fashion photography. He has been involved with the Australian Centre for Photography and works for most of Australia's leading magazines.

Ethan Hoffman   **USA**

Hoffman won the 1980 World Understanding Award for his photo essay on Washington State Prison. His work has appeared in *Life, GEO,* the New York *Times, Stern, Paris-Match* and the London Daily *Telegraph.*

Douglas Holleley   **Australia**

Holleley concentrates on photographing the Australian bush with Polaroid film. He has exhibited throughout the world and has received numerous grants and awards.

Graham Howe   **Australia**

Howe has served as Director of the Australian Center for Photography in Sydney and Curator of the Graham Nash Collection in San Francisco. Collections of his work appear in the Museum of Modern Art in New York, the Bibliotheque Nationale in Paris, and the National Gallery of Victoria.

Dallas 1976

Phil Huber   **USA**

Huber started out with UPI and then joined the Dallas *Times-Herald.* In mid-1980 he began freelancing. His work has taken him primarily throughout Mexico and Central America as well as to Europe and Asia.

Carolyn Johns   **Australia**

Johns commenced her photographic career after 10 years of nursing. Her work appears in *Newsweek,* and she also freelances for The Australian Consolidated Press and The British Film Institute. After DITLA she was assigned by the *National Times* to shoot photographs for a series of articles entitled 'Sex in Australia'.

Chris Johns   **USA**

Currently employed on the Seattle *Times* Sunday Magazine, Johns was named Newspaper Photographer of the Year by the National Press Photographer Associations in 1978.

Vietnam 1968

Phillip Jones Griffiths   **UK**

'There was an incredible hostility amongst the whites in the Dampier area towards the idea of photography, while the aboriginals were most open to it. The most intriguing character I met was a hermit priest. We sat on the beach all night long watching the jumbo jets with their in-flight movies flickering overhead. We discussed philosophy and the nature of life. It was perhaps the most pleasant evening I've spent in my life'.

Griffiths is the current president of the Magnum Photo Agency in New York. His book *Vietnam Inc.* published in 1968 had a large influence on the American withdrawal from that conflict. More recently his work has appeared in *GEO* and in the *Bangkok Book,* one of the *Time-Life* Series on the Great Cities of the World.

Han Juce   **China**

Juce graduated from the Photography Department of the Changchun Cinema College in 1963. He was then assigned to work as a staff photographer for the Xinhua News Agency and has since travelled extensively in China and overseas. Shortly after DITLA he was assigned to Xinhua's New York Bureau.

Douglas Kirkland   **Canada**
Kirkland is one of the world's best known glamour and personality photographers. His recollections of 20 years in the business portraying stars and sex symbols from Marilyn Monroe to Farrah Fawcett-Majors are soon to be published in a collection of pictures and anecdotes entitled *Offscreen*. He is one of the founding members of Contact Press Images.

Kent Kobersteen   **USA**
'The Police told me not to take any pictures of them beating up aborigines.'
A staff photographer on the Minneapolis *Tribune*, Kobersteen has covered stories on the drought and famine in the Sahel, and oil production and politics in the Middle East. He has also worked in Canada, Mexico and Cuba.

Steve Krongard   **USA**
Krongard works primarily in colour. His photographs were recently included in *Glimpses of America*—the first exhibit of American colour photography shown in the Peoples Republic of China. His advertising clients include American Airlines and British Airways.

Sara Krulwich   **USA**
Krulwich is currently working as a staff photographer for the New York *Times*. She has also worked as a staff photographer for the Philadelphia *Enquirer*.

Burma 1978

Hiroji Kubota   **Japan**
In 1970, Kubota received the first Kodansha Publishing Culture Award, given by Japan's largest publishing house. He has produced many articles on Asia for the world's press. Eight weeks after DITLA he was selected as the Japanese Photographer of the Year.

Kaku Kurita   **Japan**
Commissions from publishing houses, advertising firms, and news magazines have taken Kurita to Australia, New Zealand, North America and Europe. He currently undertakes assignments for *Newsweek* and represents Gamma Photos in Japan.

John Lamb   **Australia**
In the course of a 27 year career, Lamb's awards include: twice Australian Photographer of the year, first in the World Press Competition in Holland; twice Australian Sports Photographer, Press Photographer of the Year in 1973, and winner of the Australian Walkley Award.

Brian Lanker   **USA**
Lanker has been Director of Photography at the Eugene *Register Guard* since 1974. Prior to that he was a staff photographer at the Topeka *Capital Journal*. During that period the NPPA named him Mid-West Photographer of the Year for five straight years and also awarded him the coveted National Newspaper Photographer of the Year (1970 and again in 1976). In 1973 he received the Pulitzer Prize in Feature Photography.

Laurence Le Guay   **Australia**
Le Guay is one of Australia's most respected and travelled photographers. He opened his own studio in Sydney in 1938, specialising in magazine, industrial and fashion photography. In 1963 he was awarded the Commonwealth Medal for contributions to commercial photography in Australia.

Neil Libbert   **UK**
Libbert has photographed for most of the major British newspapers and magazines since 1958. His work has appeared in *The Guardian*, the London Sunday *Times*, and the *Observer*.

John Loengard   **USA**
One of *Life's* most distinguished staff photographers of the '60s, Loengard was included as a 'Master of the Modern Print' by the *Time-Life* Library of Photography. His guidance on the 10 *Life* Special Reports (one of them was 'One Day in the Life of America') was one of the major factors in the Magazine's rebirth in 1978.

Gerd Ludwig   **Germany**
'I was really shocked with the amount of prejudice going on. The same person who would tell you not to worry about locking the car would talk about the aborigines in a way that frightened me.'
Ludwig is a founding member of the Visum Photographic Agency. His work has appeared in *Life*, *GEO*, *Stern*, *Zeit-Magazine* and many other publications. He has won numerous awards and has contributed to exhibitions throughout the world.

JOHN MARMARAS

FORTUNE
GROWTH ROCKS
THE RECORD INDUSTRY

Three Tycoons Called the Bee Gees

What Carter's New Energy Policy Won't Do

The World According to Zbigniew Brzezinski

Momentous Legal Spillage from the "Amoco Cadiz"

John Marmaras   **Australia**
Marmaras has worked on assignments for magazines such as *Fortune*, *GEO*, *Time*, *Sports Illustrated*, the London Sunday *Times*, New York *Times* Magazine and *National Geographic*.

Harry Mattison   **USA**
'Australia was depressing at first but when I turned to the people I found as openness that was disarming, a basic feeling of integrity. It was an openness very different from what I usually feel in the States. The Australian people are latter 20th century pioneers. The restrictions of a 24 hour assignment were intriguing. It forced me to make every moment count.'
Mattison began his career as a photojournalist in 1978 covering the Nicaraguan Revolution for Associated Press and has recently devoted himself to covering the events in El Salvador. As a member of the Gamma Liaison picture agency his work has appeared in *Time*, the New York *Times*, and many major European magazines.

Stephanie Maze   **USA**
Maze has covered major international sports events including the Montreal and Moscow Olympics. As a freelance photographer she has recently worked on social issue subjects such as Mexican-American itinerant workers for *National Geographic*.

Rudi Meisel   **Germany**
Meisel is a founding member of Visum, one of West Germany's top photo agencies. Since 1975 his work has appeared in *Der Spiegel*, *Stern* and *GEO*. His assignments in East Germany were recently published as a book. His work has won numerous national and international awards.

SUSAN MEISELAS
NICARAGUA
S U S A N   M E I S E L A S
Nicaragua 1978

Susan Mieselas   **USA**
Meiselas' work has been published throughout the world. She recently won the Robert Capa Gold Medal for outstanding reportage for her coverage of hostilities in Nicaragua. Meiselas has published two books of her work; *Carnival Strippers* in 1975 and *Nicaragua* in 1981. She is a member of the Magnum Photo Agency.

Graham McCarter   **Australia**
His major assignments have included the Rolling Stones Australian and New Zealand tour, and commercial work for Coca-Cola, Cathay Pacific, UTAH Mining and Singapore Airlines. He won the New York Art Directors CLIO award in both 1978 and 1980.

ROBERT McFARLANE
Sydney 1976

Robert McFarlane   **Australia**
McFarlane has contributed to such Australian magazines as *Walkabout*, *Vogue*, *People*, *Bulletin*, *Chance*, *Australian Photography* and *Pol*, as well as serving as editor of *Camera World* for two years. During the early 1970s, McFarlane lived in Europe and his work appeared in the Sunday *Times*, *Nova*, *Car*, *Geographical* Magazine and *Man and Woman*.

Wally McNamee   **USA**
'Northwestern Australia was like southern California 30 years ago. There's a sense of hard work there. People subjected to the same problems form strong human bonds. It was good to see a willingness to cope with physical hardship to do the job. I came away with a very positive feeling.'
A veteran Washington photographer who is noted for his versatility, McNamee has covered sports, political campaigns, and movie stars. He is currently working with *Newsweek* where he has shot more than 100 cover photographs.

Dilip Mehta   **India**
Mehta was a former art director with Canadian publications and television stations. He has produced four books on India and has contributed a wide variety of stories and photographs to international magazines. Currently he is producing a major essay on the Sikh nation for *GEO* Magazine. He is associated with Contact Press Images.

Michael Morcombe   **Australia**
During 10 years as an amateur naturalist Morcombe has specialised and developed many new techniques for photographing timid and rarely seen animals in colour. His books include *Birds of Australia* and *Australia's National Parks*.

Robin Moyer   **USA**
Moyer has completed major assignments for *Time*, *Newsweek*, *GEO*, *Smithsonian*, and *Science 80*. His work is included in the 'Masters of Photography' collection at the Library of Congress. He is associated with the Black Star Photo Agency.

Matthew Naythons   **USA**
'There is more wildlife within a kilometre of my house in Sausalito than there is on the whole island I was assigned to. The only wildlife was two pelicans, both of which had names'.
Naythons spends half his time working as a photojournalist covering wars, revolutions, disasters, and plagues. He spends the other half treating the victims of those disasters as a physician. Associated with the Gamma Liaison Picture Agency, Naython's work has appeared in *Time*, *Newsweek*, *Stern*, *Paris-Match*, and the Sunday *Times*. In 1979 he founded an emergency medical team to care for Cambodian Refugees and displaced Thai villagers.

Michael O'Brien   **USA**
O'Brien has won two Robert F. Kennedy Journalism Awards for outstanding coverage of the disadvantaged. He was cited for the World Understanding Award given by the National Press Photographic Association. His work appears frequently in *Life* and *GEO*.

Max Pam   **Australia**
Pam's work is represented in the collections of the Victoria and Albert Museum, the State Gallery of South Australia and the French Bibliotheque. His one-man shows have appeared at the Aspects Gallery, Brussels, the Fremantle Art Centre and the Panagia Club, Borneo. In 1981 he was nominated as one of the *Time-Life* Photographer Discoveries of the Year.

Andy Park   **Australia**
Park is one of the two directors of '*A Day in the Life of Australia*'. Australian-born and American-educated, he returned to Melbourne seven years ago. Park originally trained as an ecologist, but began freelancing as a photojournalist soon after arriving back in Australia. He has travelled extensively throughout Australia while on assignment for *Time*, *GEO*, *Smithsonian*, *Pol*, *Parade* and *People* magazines.

Bill Pierce   **USA**
Pierce's work has been published in virtually every major journal in the world. Currently a contract photographer with *Time-Life*, he recently won the World Press competition with a colour series entitled 'The Brain'.

Bruce Postle   **Australia**
With 25 years experience as a press photographer in Australia, Postle's thousands of assignments have ranged from skydiving to accompanying oil rig divers to ocean depths. His awards include firsts in news, sports, general and portrait categories, and best series of photographs in both the Nikon and Rothmans National Press Photographer competitions.

Phillip Quirk   **Australia**
Quirk specialises in reportage photography. He has had numerous exhibitions of his work including the Inaugural Exhibition at the opening of the Australian Centre for Photography in 1974 and the Philip Morris Trust Exhibition.

Irvin Rockman   **Australia**
Rockman, a former Lord Mayor of Melbourne, is one of Australia's leading underwater photographers. He is currently working on his second book, *Love of the Sea*.

Sebastian Salgado   **Brazil**
'*Australia is not a real country for me. I got no feeling of its culture. I've never seen a country as big as this with no people inside it.*'
Associated with the Sygma, Gamma and Magnum photo agencies, Salgado's work has been seen in *Time*, *Newsweek*, the New York *Times* Magazine, and *Stern*.

David Segal   **Australia**
Segal's first major assignments were with Australian book and magazine publishers, but recently he has been working for *Life* and *Time* Magazines. His assignments have taken him to Europe, Israel, USA and New Guinea.

Sydney 1978

Roger Scott   **Australia**
Scott's work can be seen at the Australian National Gallery, the National Gallery, the Art Gallery of New South Wales and the Bibliotheque in Paris. He was awarded a Visual Arts Board grant in 1975.

Vladimir Sichov   **Stateless**
Sichov emigrated from the USSR to France in 1980, bringing with him his photo archives. These photographs have since appeared in major international magazines. Through *Paris-Match* he published a book called *Les Russes*.

Robyn Davidson 1978

Rick Smolan   **USA**
'*A Day in the Life of Australia*' project was originally conceived by Smolan, an American photojournalist who has worked extensively in Asia and Australia for the past five years. His work has appeared in major news and feature magazines including *Time*, the London Sunday *Times*, *Stern*, *Bunte*, *Oggi*, the New York *Times*, *Newsweek*, *Life*, *People*, *Fortune* and *National Geographic*. He is one of the founding members of Contact Press Images.

Wesley Stacey   **Australia**
Stacey is best known for his photographic documentation of the Australian environment, architectural history and for his recording of aboriginal culture and heritage. His photographs appear in the National Gallery of Australia, the National Gallery of Victoria, the National Gallery of NSW and in many private collections.

Terry Straight   **Australia**
'*What hurt the most was seeing the way aboriginal art and history had been vandalised.*' Straight has 19 gold and 44 silver awards for his advertising work. His clients include nearly all the major international advertising agencies and companies such as Mount Isa Mines, Coca Cola, Nestles, Comalco, CSR and the Queensland Tourist Authority.

Shomei Tomatsu   **Japan**
Tomatsu has won many awards for his work including the Education Minister's Art Encouragement Award for 1976. He has held one-man exhibitions

throughout Japan and has contributed to several group exhibits. His most recent exhibition—*World of Shomei Tomatsu*—was displayed throughout Japan in 1981.

Alexander Tsiaras   **USA**
'*I like Australia very much but was disappointed that it was not culturally and visually different than America. It is, after all, on the other side of the world*'. Best known for his 'human condition' photo essays, Tsiaras' work has been published in *Discover*, *Life*, *Time-Life* books, *Time*, *GEO* (Germany), *GEO* (USA), the London *Times* Magazine and *Natural History*.

Penny Tweedie   **Australia**
Tweedie is best known for her documentation of international social issues such as the Bangladesh refugees, the Indo-Pakistan war, Timor 1975, Montagnards in Vietnam and the Arab/Israeli conflict. Her many grants and awards include: British Arts Council, Australian Arts Council, and Australian Institute of Aboriginal Studies.

Neal Ulevich   **USA**
Ulevich won the Pulitzer Prize for News Photography in 1977. He covered the Vietnam conflict for Associated Press in the early 70s and later became the regional photographer and photo editor for AP. He is now head of photography operations in Asia for the AP and is based in Tokyo.

Sophia Loren 1980

Douglas Vann   **USA**
Vann's portrayal of night life, together with his ability to catch candid shots of celebrities, has earned him extensive coverage in *Time*, *Newsweek*, the New York *Post*, the New York *Daily News* and *Encore* Magazine. He is presently a staff photographer for the *Village Voice*.

John C. Walsh   **Australia**
While working as a lecturer in photography at the National Art School, Walsh produced a one-man show on urban Australia and another entitled '*Another Britain*'. He has photographed for the Australian Opera Company and has taken photomicrographs of rotifers and other minute crustaceans for publication in *National Geographic*.

Chelsea 1975

Patrick Ward   **UK**
In 1975, Ward received a Kodak bursary which resulted in the publication of *Wish You Were Here—The English at Play*. Other publications include *Flags Flying*, a record of British Jubilee celebrations, *Amsterdam*, published by *Time-Life* books and *The Bike Riders*, a study of motorcyclists. Ward recently spent a year in America on a Bicentennial Fellowship.

Alex Webb   **USA**
Webb's major studies include teenagers, Southern Evangelism, the Mississippi Delta, Southern Prisons, Haiti, Jamaica, the Mexican Border, Grenada, the Ivory Coast, Uganda and Washington DC. He has worked extensively for the New York *Times* and *GEO*. He is a member of the Magnum Photo Agency.

Vermont 1972

Ulrike Welsch   **Germany**
'*One policeman in the Nullarbor region was responsible for an area of 134,000 km². Probably the biggest beat in the world!*'
Welsch's various assignments have included the Robert Kennedy funeral and school desegregation in Boston. She prefers to concentrate on everyday human interest stories. In 1974, she was the New England Press Photographer of the Year.

Richard Woldendorp   **Australia**
A freelancer for national Australian magazines, Woldendorp has undertaken several overseas commissions and also has worked for mining companies during the mining boom. A one-man exhibition of his work was held in Australia in 1976 and his work has appeared in numerous books.

Cary Wolinsky   **USA**
Wolinsky has covered the world from Wisconsin to India as a freelancer for *National Geographic* and other publications. From 1968 to 1973, he worked as a staff photographer for the *Boston Globe*. Since then, he has had several group and one-man shows. He is associated with the Stock Boston Agency.

Milton Wordley   **Australia**
Wordley joined *The Australian* in 1971 and became Assistant Picture Editor in 1974. Between 1975 and 1976, he travelled in Europe and Asia then freelanced in London covering the Australian Cricket Tour. During this time his pictures appeared in the *Daily Express*, *The Guardian* and the *Daily Mirror*. He is now based in Adelaide.

Teresa Zabala   **USA**
'*Perth has a real boom town atmosphere. If I come back in say 10 to 15 years I will be glad to have seen Perth today*'.
Zabala is a Washington-based staff photographer for the New York *Times*. She has covered the last three consecutive Presidential administrations; Ford, Carter and Reagan.

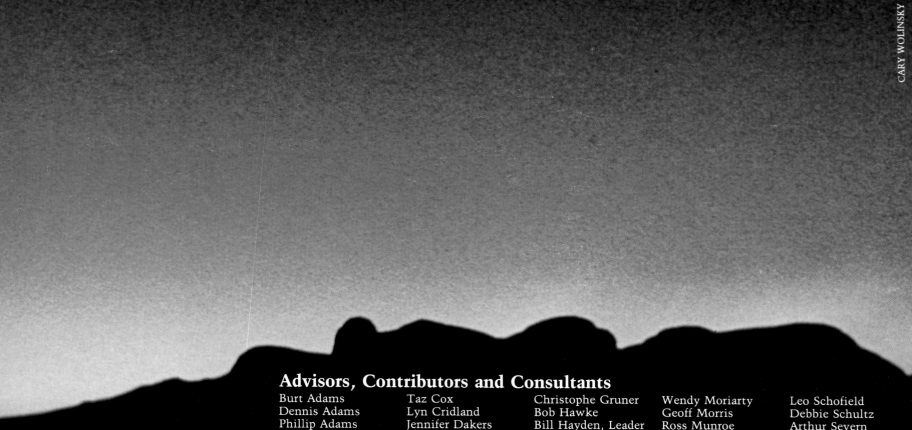

DITLA Staff Members
Directors: Rick Smolan and Andy Park
Business Manager: Joyce Childress
Office Manager: Michelle Beaumont
Project Co-ordinator: Lyne Helms
Project Manager: Mary Jean Stewart
Production Assistants:
  Lorraine Minter
  Fay Goodchild
  Françoise Kirkland
  Gina Maniaci

State Co-ordinators
Queensland: Margaret Clift
Western Australia: David Cohen
Victoria: John Marmaras
Northern Territory: Ian McIntosh
South Australia: Ian Page
Tasmania: Tony Salisbury
New South Wales: Story Shem

Co-ordinator USA: Ben Friedman

Office Staff
Dee Foster
Sebastian Gollings
Rosemary Ingram
Jackie Mott
Anton Starc
Dennis Starc
Leanne Temme

Caption Writers
Margaret Clift
Fay Goodchild
Julien Greig
Cher Humphries
Andy Park
Rick Smolan

Picture Editors
Dorean Davis (Newsweek)
Steve Ettlinger (GEO Magazine)
Terry Le Goubin (Colorific)
Michael Rand (London Sunday Times)

Design and Production
Designer: Adrian Young
Design Assistant: Susie Agoston
Cartographer: Winifred Mumford
Colour Consultant: Leslie Smolan
Tokyo Colour Assistance:
  Yukihiro Kamaishi
Printing Assistance:
  John Stewart   Karen Tucker
  Jim Stockton

Printing at Griffin Press Limited
Don Bolt   Graham Nancarrow
Michael Brown   Max Richards
Trevor Clements   John Roach
Peter Dempsey   Ted Sbisa
John Griffith   Bob Searle
Martin Horsman   Don Stewart
Barry McDermott   Bernie Wang
Ray Mules

A special thanks to John Coleman and
John Malone of the Australian
Information Service, Canberra.

Advisors, Contributors and Consultants

Burt Adams
Dennis Adams
Phillip Adams
Christine Ahnfeldt
Rocco Alberico
Elizabeth Alexander
Trevor Alfred
Ian Anderson
Alex Anisimoff
Frank Ball
Peter Banki
Ed and Rena
  Barnum
Richard Bernstein
Robin Binder
Trish Blunt
David Boward
Peter Browne
Graham Brooke
Phil Burford
Eric Butterfield
Bob Buxton
Peter Bycroft
Diane Calder
Allan Callighan
Jane Cameron
Woodfin Camp
Sharon Campbell
Ross Campbell-Jones
Alan and Adrienne
  Carroll
Val Carter
Anne and John
  Chapman
Tom Chapman
Suzanne Charlé
Fumiya Chiba
Patrick Clarke
Andree Clift
Josephine Clift
Megan Clift
Sheyne Clift
Jill Clout
Ken Cobbledick
Freda Colbourne
Danny Collins
Graham Cook
Cherie Connally
Charles Constance
Guy Cooper
Sir Charles Court

Taz Cox
Lyn Cridland
Jennifer Dakers
Brian Dale
Tom David
Robyn Davidson
Andrew Dawson
Chris Denegris
Peter Dickinson
Peter Dinham
Geoff Dixson
Arnold Drapkin
Ian Drennan
John and Mick
  Drury
Alistair Drysdale
William T. Duggan
John and Eileen
  Dunn
John Durniak
Mollie Dyer
Jim Eames
David Ednie
Kathy Enders
Chief Minister
  Paul Everingham
Bill Finke
Iain Finlay
Mike Finn
Kerry Fischer
Billie and Michael
  Fitzgerald
Ted Fitzgerald
Gary Foley
Jenny Foley
Glen Forbes
Bud and Trish Ford
Frank Fournier
Rea Francis
Gay Franklin
Wally Franklin
Rt. Hon. J.M. Fraser,
  Prime Minister
Chris Fryman
Jim George
Christine Godden
George Goldberg
Yosse Goldberg
Harry Gordon
Greaterix Family
Peter Greenberg

Christophe Gruner
Bob Hawke
Bill Hayden, Leader
  of the Opposition
Sue Haynes
Roland and Sue Hill
Philippa Hintz
Geoff Hiscock
Maurice Holland
Cher and Alan
  Humphreys
Herschell Hurst
Iris Jacobson
Doc Jardene
Pamela Kelly
Kevin Kerr
Geoff Kirk
Phillip Knightley
Janice Koch
Phil Kunhardt
J.P. and Eliane
  Laffont
Jim Lane
Ted Latter
Jürgen Lawrenz
Terry Lee
John Leggo
Claire Leimbach
Arnold Levenberg
Leila Levy
Ton Linsen
Kerrie Lockwood
Heather MacDonald
Ian and Denise
  MacIntosh
Duffy Maclean
Peter McDonald
Ranald McDonald
Rod McDowell
Kathy McLaughlin
Amanda McNamara
Tony Maine
Alma Mainwaring
Steve Mark
Ian Matthews
Glyn May
Richard Mellott
Bobby Merritt
Anne Meurant
Tony Mina
James Moore

Wendy Moriarty
Geoff Morris
Ross Munroe
John Murphy
Peter Murphy
Jay Murray
Collin Myers
Koh Nagasue
Steve Neale
John Newfong
Merri Nicholson
Lee Nuss
Eva Nutt
Cathy and Paul
  Oberle
Dan O'Keefe
Bill Ouwens
Peter Owens
David Page
Annette Palaez
Nick and Ann Park
Ted and Jean Park
Lisa and Joe
  Park/Janovitch
John Paton
Premier Joh Bjelke-
  Petersen
Brian Pilbeam
Euan Pizzey
Robert and
  Catherine Pledge
Eric Poole
Ken Prentice
Jan Ralph
Wal Reid
Spencer Reiss
John Ridley
Wendy Ritchie
Ian Roache
Carl Robinson
Lois Roffey
John Ross
Tim Rossi
Helen Routh
Alfred and Pam
  Ruskin
Hugh Ryan
John Sainken
Murray and Jenny
  Sayle
Pam Seaborn

Leo Schofield
Debbie Schultz
Arthur Severn
Trish Shepperd
Peter Shilton
Philipp Short
Chris Simond
David Sinclair
Bob Siroka
Bob Smith
Max Smith
Nola Smith
Marvin and Gloria
  Smolan
Sandy Smolan
Anne Songy
Andy and Sue Speirs
Suzie Speirs
David Stewart
John Stewart
Tony Stewart
Jonathan Stone
Graham Stuart
Peter Sutch
Jim Sutton
Mark and Marion
  Swanton
Peter Tansey
Pru Taubert-Heisler
Peter Thompson
John Tilton
Neil Travers
Wyndham Venning
Sir James Walker
Aiden Wallace
Cardin Wallace
Ian and Julie Wallace
John Ward
Ian Watson
Trevor Weatherill
Kevin Weldon
Anne Wetzler
Debbie Wildman
Brian Williams
Lester Wisbroad
Shona Wood
Premier Neville
  Wran
Kaz Yamane
Trudy and Tony
  Zussino

Overseas Agents

France
Annie Boulat, Cosmos
56 Boulevard de la Tour Maubourg
75007 Paris
Phone 705 4429, Telex 203085
Germany
Marita Kankowski, Focus
Schlueterstrasse 6, 2000 Hamburg 13
Phone 44 3769, Telex 2164242
Italy
Grazia Neri, Via Senato 18, 20121 Milano
Phone 79 9275, Telex 312575

Japan
Bob Kirschenbaum, Pacific Press
CPO 2051, Tokyo
Phone 264 3821, Telex 26206
United Kingdom
Terry Le Goubin, Colorific Photo Library
Gilray House, Gloucester Terrace, London W2
Phone (01) 723 5031 or 402 9595
United States
David Cohen, Woodfin Camp
415 Madison Avenue, New York City 10017
Phone (212) 750 1020, Telex 428788

Thank you to the people of Australia

If you think getting 100 photographers to set their egos aside to work together was difficult, imagine the amount of persuasion it took to get an equal number of companies and individuals to support this project in the first place! We were extremely fortunate to find people within each corporate group who had the imagination to help turn an impossible dream into a reality. They are patrons of the arts in the true sense of the word—giving the 100 photographers complete freedom to photograph whatever they discovered during their 24-hour assignment. DITLA wishes to express thanks to each of them.

Project Sponsors

Underwriter
BP Australia

Major Subsidisers
Qantas Airways Limited
Telecom Australia
Trans Australia Airlines

Sponsors
Alcoa of Australia Limited
Associated Pulp and Paper
  Mills Limited
Australian Consolidated
  Industries Limited
Coopers & Lybrand
Hyatt Kingsgate Hotel
J. Gadsden Australia Limited
M.I.M. Holdings Limited
Monier Limited
Wesfarmers

Subsidisers
Apple Computers Inc.
Australian Information Service
Cathay Pacific Airways
Kestrel Films (Australia) Pty Ltd
Kodak (Australasia)Pty Ltd
Merrill Lynch and Associates
Philip Morris Arts Grant
Polaroid Australia Pty Ltd
Skypak International
State Bank of NSW
Vision Graphics Pty Ltd
Westpac Banking Corporation Ltd

Contributors
Airlines of New South Wales
Airlines of Western Australia
American Photographer Magazine
Arkaroola Wildlife Sanctuary
  and Resort
ASP Micro Computers
ATN Channel Seven Sydney
Australian Associated Press
Australian Land and Cattle Company
  Limited
Australian National Railways
Avis Australia
Barossa Valley Tourist Association
BHP Australia
Bush Pilots of Australia Airlines
Circus Royale
Coober Pedy Taxi Service
Department of the Chief Minister,
  Northern Territory
Department of Correctional Services,
  South Australia
East-West Airlines
Fish Marketing Authority of
  New South Wales
Flinders Hotel, Port Augusta
Grant Matthews Photography
HSV Channel Seven Melbourne
Ilford Australia Pty Ltd
JBG Photographic Lab
Life Magazine
Lindeman (Holdings) Ltd
Linnett's Island Club, Kangaroo Island
Lindsay Park Stud
New South Wales Department of
  Tourism
New South Wales Film Corporation
New South Wales State Fisheries
Northern Territory Tourist
  Commission
Oberoi Adelaide

Olivetti Australia Pty Ltd
Pics Australasia Pty Ltd
Premier's Department of
  New South Wales
Premier's Department of Queensland
Premier's Department of Victoria
Premier's Department of Western
  Australia
Queensland Tourist and Travel
  Association
Royal Australian Air Force
Royal Australian Army
Royal Brisbane Hospital
Royal Flying Doctor Service,
  Queensland
Santos Limited
Skywest Airlines
Sheraton Perth Hotel, Western
  Australia
Shirley Spectra
Time Magazine
Victorian Government Travel
  Authority
Western Australian Department of
  Tourism
Western Continental Corporation
William Booth Salvation Army
  Hostel, Adelaide
Woods and Forests Department,
  South Australia
Woodside Off-Shore Petroleum
  Pty Ltd

DITLA is especially grateful to Nikon for their generosity in providing testing facilities and supplementary equipment for the 70 photographers who used Nikon cameras during the project.